T0380615

The Gift

The Gift

KRIS VALLAY

ARCHWAY
PUBLISHING

This book is a work of non-fiction. Unless otherwise noted, the author and the publisher make no explicit guarantees as to the accuracy of the information contained in this book and in some cases, names of people and places have been altered to protect their privacy.

Archway Publishing books may be ordered through booksellers or by contacting:

Archway Publishing
1663 Liberty Drive
Bloomington, IN 47403
www.archwaypublishing.com
1 (888) 242-5904

Because of the dynamic nature of the Internet, any web addresses or links contained in this book may have changed since publication and may no longer be valid. The views expressed in this work are solely those of the author and do not necessarily reflect the views of the publisher, and the publisher hereby disclaims any responsibility for them.

Any people depicted in stock imagery provided by Getty Images are models, and such images are being used for illustrative purposes only. Certain stock imagery © Getty Images.

Editor – Sonita Singh
Proof reader – Sarah Collisson

ISBN: 978-1-4808-6549-5 (sc)
ISBN: 978-1-4808-6550-1 (e)

Library of Congress Control Number: 2018951430

Print information available on the last page.

Archway Publishing rev. date: 10/20/2018

This book is dedicated to my amazing boys. It is because of you I know what true joy feels like.

#MikeyMonday
Me: Mikey, I love you. Not just a little bit. I mean I really love you a lot.
Mikey: Ok
Me: How do you feel about me?
Mikey: I don't know (Pause) I mean I really don't
know. (Pause) You're ok I guess.

In so many ways we are all the same. Then there are those moments, well I know I have them at least anyway, that I think, *I'm sure there is no-one on earth that lives like this.* It was in those moments of thought that I was inspired to write this book.

You see my life journey is one like no other. One that I would never imagined ever living. It's an interesting tale to say the least and one that to be perfectly honest, I now take great pride in.

Let me explain a bit about what I mean.

Years ago, a woman had no idea just how precious her life was. She was happy, but she lacked the substance in her soul that can only be borne from adversity, challenge or depression. That woman was me.

Luckily, I was to face just these things all at the same time.

I have four beautiful, vibrant, hilarious, smart, happy, focused, centered boys. Jarod, Ben, Mikey and David. They are all diagnosed on the Autism Spectrum. I am now raising them as a single mum and we love it.

There were many times that I questioned why life should be so hard. Why others seemed to be given an easier path. Why I seemed to be dealt with challenge after challenge. Heartbreak and pure despair were my two best friends for a long period of time.

From there I experienced glimpses of a better life, a better way of thinking and being. From my children, I eventually learnt what pure joy feels like. The real story here is my journey in the pursuit of joy. How I discovered my 'happy place'.

It comes, at times, from very dark places, and other times seemingly neutral or unimportant events. There were many times I wanted to give up and throw in the towel. I wanted to curl up and sleep till I was dead. It was my children that always got me out of bed and if I am to be honest here, it was also the fear of judgment from other mums. What if they saw me as a 'bad mother'?

I made one small decision after another to show up. To be present. To focus on the children's needs and not societies views. To make up my own mind. To throw out the social rule books that bound me. To love unconditionally from the deepest place in the soul of my being.

I discovered that Autism is a gift. It was the best thing that has ever happened in my life. I feel so blessed and honoured to have been granted the opportunity to experience it through my children.

I live the belief that it doesn't matter what life throws our way, we can always choose bliss if we are looking for it. We choose how we feel about our life. What you focus on expands.

There was a long stretch where I honestly don't remember feeling much at all. I called it my 'robot phase'. One situation after another led to this feeling of apathy. I trudged between appointments, diagnoses and therapy. Life on 'auto pilot' was a definite coping mechanism that served me for many years.

It's been a rollercoaster ride for sure. There were many times that if I hadn't been strapped in, I might have ejected my seat and got right out of there. I'm so glad that I did stay and held on for the ride.

As this book is sent to the publisher, my oldest son Jarod is studying Information Technology at the local University. Ben is studying Science and Commerce at a University in Melbourne, living independently on his own. Both Jarod and Ben have part time jobs mentoring kids with

Autism in schools. Mikey attends the nearby Specialist School and just got offered a part time job at a local supermarket. David attends High School and loves creating new board games and expressing himself through his art. The book's cover was drawn by David; showcasing what his visual representation of Autism is. It's a perfect encapsulation of the contents.

The following is a series of snapshots of things that have happened in our lives and what lessons I took from them. There are some things I have left out to respect the privacy of my boys, but on the whole, I think it's a good overview of just how whacky and wonderful your life can become if you choose it. The unique way my kids look at life is definitely worth exploring further. The stories are not in any particular order.

I thought that was an appropriate reflection of what life is like with Autism. Things don't tend to happen in a perfect sequence.

The Mikey Monday quotes started a few years after Mikey developed speech (he started to speak in sentences at the age of 8). Capturing those precious words coupled with a very unique mindset has been important on so many levels for us all.

#MikeyMonday
Mikey comes into my room and flops his head on my bed.
Me: You look tired. What time did you get up this morning?
Mikey: I woke up at 7. I'm not tired, my body is fine.
I'm just waiting for my head to catch up.

From three months old my first son Jarod would smile at everyone and anyone that paid him attention. Walking in the pram, he would smile at every single person that walked past. I was so proud.

His first few years were filled with instances of Jarod being polite to those around him. He was a rule follower and responded well to direction and guidance. Jarod learnt very quickly what was expected of him in terms of behaviour and he responded well. A model son.

The first time around motherhood was a breeze for me. Jarod slept well, he fed well, and he behaved well. I worked part time and loved it.

Ben came along unexpectedly seventeen months later. Ben was different. I was different. My husband was studying at University and as such, I needed go back to working full time to support the family when Ben was only sixteen weeks old. Ben screamed day and night. We went through many tests and theories as to why he just wouldn't settle. Foods I was eating, then his formula – soy based or goat's milk, all the things that a mother tries to solve the puzzle.

Times were tough, and I wasn't coping. My second day back at work I was called away after Jarod had an accident in the pram. He had to be rushed to hospital to have three of his front teeth removed.

I sat and breastfed Ben in the hospital whilst holding Jarod, screaming for my cuddles and blood dripping from his mouth over my breasts. I didn't cry. I was so overwhelmed that I don't remember feeling anything at all.

It didn't take long after that for the cracks to show. My lack of sleep from Ben's constant screaming came to a head when I just couldn't function at work. I developed physical symptoms that stemmed from my anxiety and I knew I needed to make changes.

I borrowed money from my parents and I went back to working part time. I put a plan in place to move closer to my work, so the travel time wouldn't cut into the time I could spend with my two boys.

When Ben was eight months old, we all moved into my current home at Mirboo North. A beautiful country town with rolling green hills, filled with wonderful welcoming people. I was devastated. In fact, two days in, I found myself in such a state of panic, that I couldn't breathe while I was in the house. I needed to go outside to calm down. I lost my ability to eat, sleep and my bodily functions were all shot. I shut down in every way possible.

My regret at having moved was extreme. I was consumed with the idea that I had made the biggest mistake of my life and that I was a terrible person for having talked my husband into going in the first place.

Unable to function myself there was no way I could take care of my two boys. I took a couple of weeks off work with sick leave. My husband was studying for exams at the time and needed to focus on that. I went with the boys to my parents' house.

Out of pure desperation, I saw their local doctor. "You are suffering from post-natal depression." He was so clear. He then asked the hardest question I've ever chosen to answer honestly.

"Do you feel the same way about Ben as you do about Jarod?"

The answer was no. I didn't. That was the first time I had ever admitted it. The shame opened up and swallowed me whole.

I was so lost I couldn't even see the doctor in front of me. I remember him saying I would feel better again if I took these pills. I didn't really believe him fully, but I didn't really feel I had a choice either given the circumstances. I was a twenty-six-year-old woman who could no longer take care of her children.

A grown woman who needed her mummy to take her to the doctor.

To my surprise and delight I did start to feel better after four days. The fog started to lift and my thoughts, slowly but surely, became more coherent and realistic. Six weeks later I felt like myself again. The doctor told me depression was a chemical imbalance and the anti-depressants were there to correct that. My views about depression before that were that it was something I should be able to control and snap out of. It wasn't for me.

The best part about that time was that the bond I had had with Jarod was developing with Ben. I grew to love him with such ferocity and deepness that in some ways I had overcorrected the prior imbalance. I think I favoured him a little for a time.

At the age of two, I remember taking Ben to his regular check up with the Maternal and Child Health Nurse. I told her he didn't speak at all. He had no words. In fact, he had spoken earlier on and then chose to stop after a few months. She said it was odd and referred me to see a speech therapist. I went home and had a few discussions with people around me. I convinced myself that it was not odd and in fact perfectly normal. I rationalised it by saying that Jarod's language had also been somewhat delayed, and that everyone develops skills at their own pace.

That was the first of many times I chose to see things from my own unique perspective. I chose denial. I chose to say that he was 'fine' on the surface and let my fears fester underneath.

Ben was very different to Jarod. He didn't seem to understand what was required of him. He would run off, not come when he was called and ignored my requests for everything. Ben was 'in his own little world'.

Ben's attention span was phenomenal. He could sit and stare for hours. I chose to see those things as blips in between all the things he didn't/wouldn't do for me in public. I feared judgment from other mums because he didn't listen and wouldn't respond. I feared that I was a 'bad mother'.

Life was full on. I was twenty weeks pregnant with my third boy Mikey. Jarod was four and Ben was two-and-a-half years old. I distinctly remember a conversation with a friend at the time, reflecting perfectly my current mindset and circumstances. She said, "Well that gives you twenty weeks to whip Ben into shape then".

I agreed with her. I was ashamed that I had been such a bad mother, others had noticed. The only saving grace I had for myself at the time, was that Jarod was a 'good boy'.

There were many times I chose to see Ben's behaviour as naughty and defiant. Ben would often ignore my calls for his attention. For example, his focus on tasks was so intense that if I packed up the pencils at playgroup to get ready for fruit time, he would bang his head on the concrete for up to an hour until his head was covered in bruises. If I didn't make him pack them up, he would draw the same set of circles for over three hours without looking up.

Ben had no awareness of others proximity unless they encroached his space. Then he wouldn't hesitate to push them out of the way if they got too close to him. I felt a myriad of emotions about Ben. Most of all I felt overwhelmed. I couldn't believe that one parenting strategy could work so well for his older brother Jarod but was completely useless on Ben. Everything about Ben was different.

I became so frustrated and deflated every time I tried a new strategy. I desperately wanted Ben to be just like the other kids and I needed to be just like the other mums. I felt like his behaviour reflected poorly on my parenting skills and I hated myself for it. I thought having post-natal depression caused this to happen and the guilt consumed me.

At the time of Ben's third birthday I had three boys. Jarod was four, and Mikey was four weeks old.

On the day of party as people arrived, they excitedly approached Ben and wished him a Happy Birthday. They handed a gift to him, which he threw on the ground rather than opening it. When encouraged to open his gifts, he screamed. I was so embarrassed. But more so terrified that this behaviour was typical of my three-year-old boy.

My world now knew what I had suspected for some time, there was something 'different' about my boy. That was the day I knew I could no longer choose to rationalise his behaviour. He wasn't tired, hungry or sick or just 'going through a phase'.

Later that afternoon my mum and I went to our local park. Ben twice tried to escape my clutches and run across the road, with cars fast approaching. He was unaware of the potential dangers on the roads. He felt no compulsion to stay near me and the safety I thought I would represent to him.

My mum said to me, "What do you think it could be?"

I had a mixture of feelings in that one moment. First came disbelief, quickly followed by dismay, then sadness kicked in. As was usual practice for me at that time, I quickly jolted myself out of that mindset and made myself bury it. I would never let myself go to the place called depression again. I would control my emotions.

Mikey comes to get his breakfast and pauses to look at his mangled pancake.
Me: I tried to turn your pancake too early.
Mikey: Oh Ok. Just do it at the perfect time then next time.
Me: Ok good idea.

Out of the blue the thought came to me like a bolt of lightning. *Maybe he is Autistic?*

I didn't even know what Autism really was at that point, but it was a possibility.

As luck would have it, that night the Lifestyle Channel aired a ninety-minute special on Autism. I watched with complete concentration. It talked about the diagnosis, described behaviours and early intervention programs. Bells rang in my mind as I mentally ticked all the boxes with Ben. For the first time in a long time, I felt somewhat relieved. The program gave me something to concentrate on. A focus for my frustration and worry.

I called the then 'Autism Victoria' the next morning. Ben needed to be assessed. My first stop; a Paediatrician.

Luck was on my side again. He was booked in for an appointment for five days later.

I sat in the waiting room anxiously waiting our turn. I was thankful Ben was finding it difficult to be in a new environment. It made me commit to the course of action I'd chosen. He began to scream and pull my hand. He tried to get me to take him to the door and home again.

He was unable to be distracted. I was completely exhausted when it came time for us to be seen.

Fortunately, the Paediatrician had a lock on his door. Ben spent the time screaming to leave but I didn't need to constantly get up and physically stop him. The whole diagnosis discussion occurred over the constant squealing, which of course escalated. He grabbed toys and threw them across the room to express his frustration at being in this new unfamiliar environment.

The Paediatrician listened to me and observed Ben's behaviours. He got out his diagnostic criteria and we went through it in detail. He confirmed what I had expected, Ben had Autism.

Further follow up and more testing by other professionals was scheduled. But I knew that day, this was the correct diagnosis for my son.

That night I went to dinner with my girlfriends. "Well it's official – he has Autism" I announced. Silence ensued. "How do you feel about that?" my gorgeous friend asked. It was the first time since I started the process that I had stopped to ponder this. I had been so wrapped up in concern for Ben and the rest of my family that I hadn't really considered what this meant for me. I was surprised with my own answer to the question; "mostly relief".

I felt relieved that I finally had a reason for his behaviour. I was relieved that I could finally forgive myself and stop blaming myself for my son's actions. That it was not my 'crap parenting' that had led to his actions. I was relieved to have a direction to go in and relieved I could help my child. I was relieved it was Autism because of all the disabilities it intrigued me.

Throughout history many famous people have 'suffered' from Autism and this fascinated me. The idea that people like Albert Einstein or Bill Gates for example were said to have had many traits that are common on the Autism Spectrum intrigued me. People who are so famous for their abilities, could also be famous for their apparent disability too. I knew I wanted to examine this dichotomy further.

It gave me hope that my son may be able to do something great even with this 'Disability'. Despite his challenges, Ben might yet be able to contribute to society in a productive and meaningful way. Something many parents of children with 'typical development' can take for granted.

I was excited by the challenge. I had chosen to rise up and run with it as best as I could. If you had asked me at the time why something like Autism motivated me, I probably wouldn't have acknowledged that it did. Some people chose to approach me with pity. I couldn't relate to those people. At that time, I only wanted to know more about this condition. A condition that could render someone completely shut down in one area but make them mind blowingly brilliant in another.

I look back at that time with gratitude. It was an emotional turning point for me. Weirdly, it was not grief that I felt. I felt like I had a purpose, a direction with which to channel my frustration and my anger. If I saw Ben's behaviour as a learning tool instead of a source of embarrassment and a reflection of my own poor parenting, I could function better. I could wake up in the morning with a renewed sense of purpose to my life. So many people around me assumed that I felt grief, *perhaps because it was what they were feeling,* and I might have just assumed I was too. To know that this was not the case empowered me, and I felt energized for what lay ahead for me.

My brain immediately kicked into overdrive. I was plagued with so many questions.

What do I do now? Where do I start? What will people say? How should we tell them? When should we tell them? What next? I asked myself the questions so fast I couldn't really consider the answers. Everything was a blur.

So, I did what I always do – I immersed myself fully in the topic (much like the special interest of an Autistic person). I joined Autism Victoria and I proceeded to read over fifty books in their library. I read texts, stories, watched DVD's, went to talks, seminars and groups on the topic. If Autism was mentioned, I wanted to know about it. I wanted to be informed. I armed myself with knowledge for both myself and my son.

Surprisingly the books that were most useful to me were not necessarily the ones the 'professionals' suggested. Some books I felt concentrated too much on examples of negative things that had happened to kids with Autism – examples of ostracism and bullying in schools, prison and physical abuse.

I guess the idea of these resources was to promote awareness and understanding of those diagnosed with Autism. I found the information defeatist, depressing and not beneficial at all. It was doom and gloom. I wanted positivity. I wanted strategies. I wanted stories of success and achievement. I wanted information on how to help my child. I needed to believe that I could make a difference in my child's life despite the circumstances. I didn't want to know about the 'bad' things that could happen.

It would have been better if that information was not available to me when Ben was first diagnosed. It didn't help with my immediate strategies for his ongoing safety. It just took up too much room in my ever-growing headspace, known as fear and worry.

I could only deal with my situation, my family and my son. I was not in any position, physically or emotionally, to deal with the global issues created by lack of awareness and understanding of Autism. I felt I was helpless to do anything about these.

I was at my own maximum coping capacity. My learning was steep, and I focused on why Ben's Autism would direct him to change his clothes if he got two drops of water on them. Or why he needed to do his wees half in one toilet and half in another. These are examples of what frustrated and fascinated me about his diagnosis.

The best books I read were written by people with Autism – children especially. They provide so much insight into the mind of Autism. I looked at what they achieved and felt empowered. Their stories filled me with hope for our future.

After a few months of investigating, I made the conscious decision to only read information that inspired me and helped our journey. I wouldn't read anything from a negative or uninspired perspective. For example, at the time Autism became a label, there was a predominant thought in the medical arena that it was caused largely because the children's mothers were 'non-caring' and 'not loving enough' and that was the reason their children 'became' Autistic. I didn't read anything that involved that theory.

Therapy was my middle name. If it was available, I'd tap into it. If it was close by, that was a bonus. I was willing to travel anywhere that would help my son on his journey. Everything I read and everyone I spoke to in the field, told me that the early years were the critical ones. I wasn't going to waste a second. Therapy officially was to help Ben engage and deal with the world he had found himself in. Unofficially, it was my chance to talk to all the other mums that were dealing with similar issues. It was my chance to learn from the professionals. To get information on how they dealt with behaviours. How they approached meltdowns with this quiet calm that I had nowhere near yet mastered.

My days were all structured from start to finish. My life revolved around the next appointment, speech therapy, group therapy, special needs playgroup etc. Ben was enrolled in all the best programs at the time.

#MikeyMonday
Jarod: Mum why are you wearing high heels?
David: She's breaking them in
Mikey: She's not breaking them in. She's so fancy that's how she rolls!

Mikey's diagnosis was the hardest. When he was two years old, I had gone to the Paediatrician for a follow up appointment to do with his bowed legs. I mentioned in passing that he had some 'Autistic like' tendencies. A phrase used to describe kids who have unusual behaviours, when we don't want to say the actual words themselves. I preferred 'tendencies', because it meant that it wasn't really Autism. It was more like some 'similar eccentricities' that he might grow out of in time. I was again referred to a specialist for his opinion. Mikey's favourite activity was banging two objects together. He often held his hands over his ears. He would hit, head butt and bite others for no apparent reason. He ignored other children including his brothers.

The specialist listened to me very carefully taking notes as I talked. Mikey sat on the floor playing with the Blu-Tack I took with me everywhere. It kept him busy and occupied when we went to a new place, so he wouldn't scream the place down.

The memory of the specialist placing the pen down onto his notes with an audible click, will be etched in my soul forever. He looked up at me with empathetic eyes and slowly asked "Why do you have any doubt?"

A long pause ensued, and it was me who babbled. "Well I guess I was just hoping it wasn't true somehow". I then looked down to my bulging belly and asked. "What are the statistics for a third child with Autism after the first two were diagnosed?". He replied, "You don't want to know the answer to that particular question."

He was right. I didn't want to know.

I left the appointment and the drive home was spent in uncomfortable silence, wondering how I could have believed Mikey was developing typically. I had decided that another child would be okay because of this. I obviously didn't wait long enough for the behaviours to present themselves. Or I just denied they existed when they were there. I had then found myself in the difficult position. I was raising two young children with Autism; one typical boy, and a baby was due to be born four weeks later. *What have I done, getting pregnant again now?*

When I got home that afternoon, I spent many hours just watching my son play. I wondered how I could have been in such denial. He literally ate books. I bought one packet of Blu-Tak for him every week, so he could roll it into balls over and over again. He said no words at all. He screamed when he wanted something.

I found it much harder to swallow this diagnosis for many reasons. Largely, I felt guilty that I'd gotten pregnant again thinking Mikey wasn't Autistic. I knew just how much work was involved in getting Ben to the point he was at, and I would need to do that again for Mikey with a newborn in tow.

A newborn that just might be Autistic too.

I don't remember crying at all. I think my 'robot phase' had well and truly kicked in then. I was all about the kids and what I could do for them. Underneath there was an intense grief. I just pushed it down, ignored it and functioned around it. I didn't want to feel guilt or regret my choices. I believed that I didn't have the time to feel it. That I needed to be consistent, reliable and available for my children. They would not have coped with a weeping mother who reacted differently to every situation. They wouldn't understand. It would have made them anxious and more violent. As it was Ben had hit me every time he was overwhelmed, or something happened that wasn't the way it was 'supposed' to be. Mikey was very much still in this phase. He struck and bit me constantly when he wanted something, and I didn't know or couldn't work out what it was.

I was unable to ever leave Mikey in the same room as baby David for fear he may step on him. Mikey did not realise he would or could do that. I showered while my husband was home. I even took David to the toilet with me when I needed to go. The house was locked up like Fort Knox, so Mikey couldn't escape. At home, he was safe and mostly happy. This was a safe haven to return to after all our appointments and sessions. Mikey found contact with people distressing. His reaction was to spend a lot of time hitting and punching me as punishment for making him experience the atrocity that was human contact.

I have many memories of strapping both Mikey and David firmly into the pram, so I could hold Ben by the arm and walk him to kinder. I'd leave Mikey and David out the front while I ran Ben in and quickly returned to take them home. Mikey was safer in the pram than out of it due to his wandering tendencies. I couldn't take the pram or him inside due to him screaming at the sight of all the people. I used to laugh to myself when I thought about what the other parents must think of me leaving two kids outside on their own, rather than bring them inside. In the pram Mikey was unable to lean over and 'swipe' David in the face because he was too far away.

I knew I just had to go with my gut on raising my children. Nothing else worked. I was the only one who had all the information about the needs of my children and this meant doing things differently to the other parents around me.

#MikeyMonday

Driving Mikey to school we go past some kids walking close by.

Mikey: Don't run over them.

Me: Oh really?

Mikey: Yeah don't.

Me: Why?

Mikey: Cause it's illegal

Mikey's behaviours were much more difficult to deal with than Ben's had been. Assumedly the level of Autism and intellectual capacity had a lot to do with that. Mikey was intellectually disabled as well as Autistic. Mikey needed to watch a few movies repeatedly. I purchased up to ten copies of Ice Age just because they wore out. He would pick up and trash everything in his path. There were locks on everything in the house and God forbid if we forgot to use them.

One day I had family visiting. When they arrived, they didn't lock the door behind them. Mikey who always seemed to have an uncanny sense of these things, knew it was open. He took his leave quietly. We realised he was gone after only a short minute, but in that time, he had stripped off all his clothes and was found on the main highway just up from our house. Someone from town had grabbed him, just before he ran into an oncoming car.

My emotions were so closed off back then. It did take a near death experience for me to really feel. In very quick succession I felt terror, followed by relief, but the emotion that stayed and that I carried with me was embarrassment. I was the mother who somehow let the Autistic boy take off all his clothes and run up the street naked, almost getting himself killed in the process. I could feel many eyes on me that day. The judgment of me showed on their faces. Little did they know that there was no judgment they could have of me, that I didn't mirror in my own mind a thousand-fold. The shame of this was so great I put my head down and avoided all eye contact in public for many years.

These kinds of disappearances happened all too regularly for a diligent house locking parent. Thankfully, Mikey was always found and never hurt. When he got older, his favourite place to run to was up the road to a friend's house. I would always call her first when he went missing.

It is funny to think about how relaxed I was about the situation. Looking back at it now, it was very scary and dangerous. It was a great facade I had created. I even fooled myself at times that I no longer felt worried about things. I couldn't afford to see it any other way at the time.

One; because I would be living in a constant state of anxiety, which is unmanageable: and two; because panic never helped in dealing with the kid's issues. I needed to be calm, so they felt free to express themselves. They had enough anxiety for all of us.

To counteract and force down the growing fear that things might not be ok, that one day Mikey might actually disappear and not come back, each time I would get better locks and find better ways to keep track of his movements. This focus allowed me to set aside the fear. I locked us away in a fortress that we called home.

#MikeyMonday
Me How was school? Did you start work experience today?
Mikey Yes
Me yayayayayay
Mikey Ok. I don't need to see the you that's on crack mum

Ben went off to mainstream primary school at the age of six. That same year Mikey started his time at special needs kindergarten. I'd spent the previous year doing speech therapy and special needs playgroup with him. It was his turn to take the next step. Mikey had just turned three and exhibited much more severe behaviours than Ben had. Mikey didn't talk at all. His go to response was to scream at the top of his lungs or hit out at people.

With that in mind, Ben's schooling was a walk in the park. I met with the Principal and first year teachers at the school. We had the same discussions and planning put into place as I had for done with him for kindergarten. Ben thrived in this structured and predictable universe. Compared to what I was dealing with at the time with Mikey, this part of my mothering of Ben was relatively straightforward and manageable. Ben had already taught himself to read before he went to school and could count in digits in the thousands. Our teaching focus for him was the social side of things. Never the academic.

It took Mikey a term in kinder to learn he didn't need to cry throughout the entire session. Then another term for the teacher and I to have the strength to make him walk for himself, rather than be carried around in the relative safety of her arms. At special needs playgroup he would cry incessantly to be picked up, so he didn't have to experience the situation he was in. He could cuddle in and block the unfamiliar situations and people out. Because of this, the staff, parents and children who also attended the Centre didn't really become familiar to Mikey for some time and his anxiety remained.

At the end of the third term Mikey had started to explore his environment and even enjoyed doing some things. Mostly he would just tip things over but at least he was learning cause and effect. I could tell he was starting to like things, because the self-stimulatory behaviours he would use at home when he was excited would start to be seen at Kinder. His favourite behaviour was very quickly flapping his arms like a bird and jumping up and down on the spot. The smile on his face when he was flapping, always reminded me of what pure joy must feel like. An emotion that he felt often but escaped me for many years. I was too busy trying to get him to do things like the rest of society to notice.

It was also amazing to watch just how much Mikey was able to communicate without speaking. He was able to get his views across most of the time and learnt to do so without hitting, kicking or punching. A relief to everyone that was in contact with him. He would grab the teachers by the hand and take them to the things he wanted to play with and spend time doing. When Mikey began to enjoy his kinder environment, he was a pleasure to watch and be around. He was a happy boy with a kind heart. Mikey was always one of those kids that wore his emotions on his sleeves. So, when he became familiar with his kinder environment he embraced it fully and enjoyed every moment of the sensory experiences they offered. The activities and the structure were great for him and his happiness was evident to all those who came into contact with him.

#MikeyMonday
Mikey: Mum you really smell. You should go wash yourself.
Me: Is it my breath?
Mikey: Yep and your skin. It's disgusting!
What??!! I'm not being offensive.... it's just the most horrible smell ever.
Me: Ok Mikey.

There have been many times I have gone down different paths with the boys. The one I feel the most shame and embarrassment for is when I was involved with the Defeat Autism Now movement. I now find it hard to write about this at all. I'm so mortified I that ever 'went there'. The movement was initiated somewhere in the United States and operated under the assumption that Autism was something that could be treated and cured. It talked about making dietary and other changes in the kid's lives to 'cure' their Autism.

Why oh why did I look for a cure? To be honest I don't think I ever thought that was possible. What I did want though, was to stop feeling so reactionary to the boy's behaviour. I wanted to feel like I had some control over our lives and for things to change. I wanted an escape from the daily violent meltdowns in the house.

This mindset was strong when I looked at Autism with the philosophy that it was not a gift. It was a seemingly endless series of meltdowns, shutdowns, embarrassing, and at times humiliating, moments for me. My life was clouded in shame that I had 'gotten myself' into this situation. I was so mortified that I had chosen to have more kids that were an 'inconvenience' to society. They had cost the citizens so many tax dollars due to the extra support they needed to function in it. I didn't feel worthy of this extra help.

My kids were eight, seven, four and two and I was lost. Life was busy, and I never knew what was going to happen during each day. What I did know was that I had to get to the next appointment whether I had slept or not, whether it induced a meltdown or not, whether I really wanted to or not. I thought that life was not about me. It was about what I could do for my kids.

I wanted to be pro-active. I wanted to feel like I had control over something, and I wanted the world to know I was doing something about it. I wasn't a victim. I was a survivor.

Looking back on my emails at the time, I feel as if I'm reading from another person's perspective. This woman was so focused, so assured, and so determined. In some ways I even envy her. Also, I pity her. I envy the passion of her spirit, the commitment to her goals and her steadfast determination and never give up attitude. I pity the woman who wanted to 'fix' her children, make the Autism diminish or disappear entirely. That woman is no longer me and for that, I am immensely grateful.

At that time there was a theory that got a lot of air play in the press. It claimed that childhood immunisations could lead to Autism in children who were predisposed to it. For example, many immunisations had been prepared with chemicals like mercury. The theory was that some kids found it harder to dispel these things from their body. They then got trapped in the body and Autistic symptoms occurred as a result.

One of the things I did at that time was test the kid's hair for chemicals. I chose not to test Jarod as his Autism had not reached my attention yet. After testing, the other three boys were shown to have toxic levels of aluminium, antimony, arsenic, cadmium, lead, nickel, silver and tin. I had myself tested too as a comparison. I was significantly different in my results and was within the normal levels of all toxic elements and had minimal essential elemental deficiencies.

After the heavy metal hair test, we also did food allergy tests. The most significant impact was on Mikey. He was found to be sensitive to dairy, gluten, salicylates and some food additives. I made the huge decision to change his diet. We started the mammoth task of attempting to get him to increase the things his body needed. This, it was thought, would help to dispel the toxicity from his body. I eliminated all foods that he found difficult to tolerate.

This was a big task for three reasons. One; because there were five other members in the family that were affected by this decision. Two: because Mikey's diet had been so limited beforehand, that decreasing the options further really impacted on his food choices; and thirdly; Mikey had spent a great deal of time eating non-food items so decreasing the amount of foods he could eat, I feared, may have led to a reappearance of this behaviour.

At the time, Mikey's behaviour was such that I printed out some information from the Internet about Attention Deficit Hyperactivity Disorder. He was extremely active and constantly jumping around. He was unable and unwilling to concentrate on much else. I joked to my friends that Mikey had the most well-formed calf muscles of any small child I'd ever seen.

I took a very deep breath and began. Mikey switched to goat's milk, soy yoghurt, dairy free margarine, spelt bread and lots of popcorn. As a family, I found it too hard to feed the other children Mikey's diet. A mix was what happened mostly – the kid's lunches had gluten and dairy with gluten free evening meals.

These changes took their toll on me. I had a meltdown. For almost a week, I locked myself away at home and poured over recipe books, diet guidelines and Internet references. I was extremely stressed and very sensitive. I was more stressed about having to cook for my children, than having to deal with the Autism itself. I was incredibly overwhelmed. I had put myself under a lot of pressure to get it right, do it properly and do it now. I told myself *there was no time like the present and I was going to do this, dammit.*

If I hadn't seen it myself, I would never have believed the impact that changes in food choices can have on a child. After a few weeks of strictly adhering to the diet, Mikey began to sit sometimes, watch TV quietly, calm down and relax more. He was a whole different child. So much so, that I knew when he must have snuck some white bread and eaten it behind the couch. When he did he would spend the rest of the afternoon completely hyperactive and jumping around the house.

I often used to say to my friends, "What a sad day it is when a kid needs to steal bread and eat it behind the couch like a criminal". But that was what it was like. He would steal wheat to eat like it was a drug and loved to get his fix. It was amazing to watch and live with every day. It was incredible because never had I seen food have such an impact on anyone's behaviour. Mikey was so obviously changed internally when he consumed wheat that it displayed in manic hyperactive behaviours such as jumping on the spot for three hours at a time.

Slowly but surely Mikey's change of behaviour led to better communication. His understanding about the world around him evolved, and he became more aware of other things in his world and ours.

Ben completed the same diet for almost a month. We were intrigued that the diet had no noticeable impact on his learning, behaviour, attitude or health. Again, the paradox of Autism affecting people in different ways was highlighted in our family. Ben began a regular diet soon afterward and he progressed steadily, with no food issues at all.

I maintained this food regime for Mikey three long years. It became increasingly difficult to hide the foods Mikey was supposed to be avoiding. As he interacted more with his siblings, he resented that his ice cream and his bread was different. Eventually Mikey refused to eat most of the foods he had lived off and began a 'determined effort' to 'steal' foods containing dairy and wheat. I decided to slowly re-introduce some foods and see how it went.

I did this over a period of about six months. I started giving foods in moderation, so we could see the effects. Mikey had made so much progress with his attention and communication. I noted his behaviour was no longer as affected by the foods as he had been in the past. Over time, I relaxed completely about the diet and he began to eat like a regular boy. If I were being completely honest, I felt some relief at his foods not being so strict. However, the underlying fear that his diet would never contain foods I considered healthy for his development, would secretly haunt me for years. During that time, I had never really addressed the issue of the low levels of essential vitamins, minerals and nutrients his body needed. I had just taken out the things that had stopped him from functioning. Then re-introduced these things back in over time.

#MikeyMonday
Mikey: I'd like to see happiness all day tomorrow.

It was a regular day, with School, basketball, dinner and homework. Except that this was to be like no other day. School for Ben that day had involved a major meltdown at lunch time. Ben's teacher had 'lied', because she said he was not the winner of a game they played. Ben found it very hard to swallow, to put it mildly. Ben didn't tell me about the meltdown at school.

I didn't think anything of it, when he became upset about losing his basketball game after school. Losing was something Ben detested, and it was also something he needed to deal with. I found basketball was so good for that – winning and losing, playing in a team.

I was to find out later that it was the wrong night to introduce Ben to a new meal – roast chicken. He had eaten chicken fillets and nuggets in the past. I thought the next logical step would be the chicken itself. We had had a great deal of trouble with Ben and new foods. I had been trying with some success to introduce some new foods to his diet. Anything that wasn't dark brown, he would try at least. It was a start.

I did the usual routine of encouragement, which lead to disapproval, which led to ultimatums about trying the food before he could have dessert. I knew about his basketball loss, so didn't push it any further. Unfortunately, it was too late, and the new meal had already been the straw that broke the camel's back.

For him, that day he had lost in a game at school, lost at basketball and then was required to eat a new food. That was too much for him.

I tucked into bed that night and he began to sob. When he got like that it was hard to console him, because he is beyond reason. I'd learned from experience that the best way was to just be there and wait for it to pass. That night it didn't. I'm still surprised now at my reaction.

Ben asked me to get him a knife.

"What do you want a knife for?" I asked him.

"So I can kill myself".

"Of course you can't have a knife, now go to sleep" was my immediate answer.

To my astonishment he did just that. He went to sleep!

That day I thought, *I should have seen it coming.* This was a common thought, but this time it had more feeling somehow. I guessed it was because of the gravity of the situation. Not the situation itself, but what it represented. I was scared at how far things could go and at such a young age. *Suicide?* I was terrified that if this is what was happening now, what was there to come for him, us, our family.

Many professionals in the field of Autism had talked about how people on the Autism Spectrum often go from one to ten in a few seconds. Like an overloaded circuit. I hadn't experienced such a violent example of this overloading and then the subsequent switching off before this night.

And it was over. The next day he woke as normal and went about his usual day.

I didn't.

I can still remember my beautiful friend comforting me when she visited, and barely being able to see her as my eyes were so wet with tears.

I was glad I had accidentally handled the incident successfully. However, I was more focused on the future. *If he wants to kill himself at the age of eight over a couple of lost games in his day, what are things going to be like when he is thirteen, fifteen, eighteen, with all the things life will throw at him then? What can I do to prevent this from happening? What could I have done in the past? Sheltered him from all games? Made sure that everything he is involved in he wins?* I was somewhat comforted by the fact that there really was no obvious option, other than the path we had chosen. He needed to learn that winning and losing go hand in hand and that losing didn't have to lead to death.

Of course, to Ben it felt like death. Losing was so abhorrent to him that he would rather die than live with that sinking feeling in his stomach. He feared that feeling. Scared of the uncertainty of it. Scared of the unknown and unpredictable. It was certainly akin to death in that moment at least.

I understood all of that. It didn't make it easier to take.

Ben had been playing basketball since he was six. During that time, he was in six grand finals. He lost the first five. Out of the five, three of the losses were by only one point. They did win once.

Looking back on Ben's basketball, I have learnt many things about how to help him handle the very real pain of losing. I've learnt not to talk about it straight after it happened. I have learnt to reward him when he copes well. I've learnt to be more forgiving and allowing of his reactive behaviours on those days. It really is those little decisions that if pushed can add up to big things, but if ignored, can serve to dissipate the situation much quicker. If he doesn't take the rubbish out on a day that he loses, is a small act to accept to allow him the space he needs.

For Ben, learning to lose has been an important life lesson and one I would never want to avoid. I am glad he finally got to experience the feeling of a medal attached to a blue ribbon around his neck though. After all that drama I asked him how he felt on the night he won and he said, "It feels good but not as much as I thought it would."

#MikeyMonday
David: I'm gonna be a sweet, rich loner when I'm older.
Mikey: No, you are not. You will be just a sidekick David.

It was October 2005. David was only twenty months old. He was very young to be diagnosed, but I was sure. The day after he turned one was the first time I 'lost' him. I had been so happy on his first birthday. Happy that I'd made it through the year with all its challenges. Happy that David responded to his name, pointed, smiled at us and was interested in people.

The very next day it all changed.

David was playing in the toy room with some toys when I called him. When I had no response, I called him louder a few more times. There was no reaction at all, he just kept playing. My gut churned, and I knew then what had happened. Autism had taken my boy. I proceeded to spend the next two months 'testing' him to be sure. Sure enough, he lost the ability to point, he lost interest in people and he no longer had any words he had used to communicate to us. Autism had hit us again. I felt numb.

I drove to the appointment with the diagnosis made in my head. I had researched Autism so fully and with such attention to specific details that I felt I knew as much as many of the professionals I worked with.

Autism is a diagnosis made after careful consideration of behavioural and environmental factors. The diagnosis is made after surveillance and through observational testing. It isn't made with a blood test and a chemical panel. I had seen it all before, many times. I knew what they would be looking for and I knew it was there. This was a formality.

My main thoughts revolved around knowing that I would cope with this one. I would choose to commit the same time and resources to David that I did for the others.

The Paediatrician didn't take much time to talk to us. He had our family history and knew why we were there. He assessed David who responded appropriately for a child with Autism. He had no speech, no gesture and rarely responded to his name. His play involved watching the same television programs repeatedly. He ignored other people and didn't make any meaningful eye contact. He didn't come to us for cuddles even when he was distressed. There was a lack of what the doctor referred to as 'interpersonal communication'.

The Paediatrician agreed with the diagnosis I had already given my child months earlier. Unlike the drive home from Mikey's diagnosis, I was not unhappy or sad. I drove home predominantly thinking about what I felt like for lunch. I guess at that time it was more 'normal' for me to have the experience of Autism than it was anything else. I'd been to so many appointments for assessments, referrals, therapy and reports that this visit was just another 'session' for me. I'd already decided David had Autism and so wasn't emotionally connected to the outcome of the appointment.

I had learned to rely on my own judgment. So, the appointments didn't hold the same significance to me that they had in the past. I didn't need anyone else to confirm my biggest fears. I could confirm them all by myself. I'd been through the fear part at home when the behaviours started. I'd done my own analysis and felt my gut clench every time he didn't respond when I called him. I'd attempted to engage David in play. Every time he was unable to connect with me was another opportunity to take a deep breath, feel the devastation for an instant, then pick myself up and take care of my boy.

By the time the appointment came, the devastation was gone and was replaced with the practical me. *What can I do now to help my son?*

When David was born, I was already attending playgroup and therapy sessions for kids with special needs. David came along to those appointments for Mikey, so it flowed easily when David was able to attend on his own. I often say David experienced the earliest intervention ever, because he had never known any different. In Autism circles, the professionals often speak about the therapy before the child attends school being the most important to their future development and their ability function well in the world. I was confident with David he had access to the best in this department because he effectively had it from birth and knew no different.

#MikeyMonday
Jarod: I'm glad you aren't having any more kids.
I don't want another brother or sister.
Mikey: I don't want another sister, but I'd like another brother.
Me: Why another brother?
Mikey: Just to have a spare one, like a spare tyre in the car.

The year Jarod (my eldest) started grade four, I started to have these mind 'clicks' concerning him and his behaviour. Things Jarod said or did would remind me of how the other boys would think.

He had increasing difficulty in social situations and he felt he was being bullied at school. Another child might tease him and call him 'shorty Phillips' and he would decide they were bullying him. He would think in extremes. To him, teasing felt like bullying because he felt the same fears as a result. I was only ever given half of the story from him. I often wondered, just what had happened in the playground?

Jarod just didn't seem to 'get it'. Life was difficult for him to read. A few family members had been in my ear for a few years about Jarod's eccentricities. I had always put it down to him being so close to Ben that he had learned some of his behaviours.

By the time Jarod was nine, it was blatantly obvious to me that he fit on the Spectrum too.

Jarod was more interested in things than people, he could become aggressive at times, he had meltdowns and was incredibly stubborn.

Jarod needed to win during games and would give up easily if he couldn't see that happening.

Jarod's diagnosis was different from the others for many reasons. Firstly; I waited two years after I had decided he had Autism to have him formally diagnosed. Secondly; because I was required to meet new professionals who we hadn't dealt with before because of his age. The other boys were all diagnosed in preschool, and as such, I utilised the services of the people we were already working with to perform the speech and psychological assessments.

Jarod was doing well in school academically and so I didn't see the need for a formal diagnosis, until it was time to prepare for high school. I was informed that Jarod might have the opportunity to receive funding for secondary school with a formal diagnosis. I did it for that reason only.

Indicative of how casual these diagnoses were becoming; my husband chose not to attend these appointments. There was no emotional attachment to them. I had already decided myself and for both of us, and it was just a matter of several pieces of paper confirming what we already knew. My husband went to work, and I went to the appointments. We had learned over time that our lives were in 'manage mode'. We scheduled in what appointments we had, and he fitted in work around it. It worked well on a practical level. I don't remember having any ill feelings toward him or our relationship at the time.

The Paediatric appointment was exactly as I expected. Probably Autism, but that we needed to have a Psychologist and Speech Therapist collaborate to complete the assessment.

For the next few months I took Jarod to about half a dozen appointments, all of which required us to drive about an hour and a half to get there. Jarod was described as 'cognitively able' but 'emotionally less mature' than his peers. His intelligence quota was described as 'superior'. Jarod was assessed as 'Mildly Autistic'. His communication and daily living skills were in the 'normal' range, however his socialisation skills were well below.

Jarod would do things like repeat "mum" over and over again, for extended periods of time, until he got my attention. If he wanted help, he would expect assistance immediately and would get angry if he had to wait. Jarod would not use non-verbal cues or gestures. He would often ask questions about the 'plan' or 'schedule' for the day, but not other questions like 'why' or 'how'.

Jarod would either give too much detail when asked about something e.g. tell me every single thing that happened in an episode of the Simpsons, or not enough information, like what had happened in the playground at school. He did not express his emotions verbally but did so instead through his behaviour. He had difficulty with sarcasm and metaphors and often asked that to be explained to him. He was unable to resolve an argument with his brothers. I would have to intervene before things got violent. He targeted his siblings regularly choking or hitting them to relieve his frustrations with the world. He avoided talking to adults he didn't know well. He sometimes came across as being rude when interacting with them, as his answers were always short and direct. He always dominated conversations about his favourite topics and was not interested in talking much at all if it was a topic he wasn't interested in. He would just stop talking if he wasn't engrossed. He always spoke in a loud voice and he didn't adjust the volume based on where he was, or who he was talking to.

Jarod's teacher confirmed that he couldn't 'read' other emotions and couldn't tell when others were being annoyed by him. Jarod's teacher also stated that Jarod would play with children three years younger than him in the playground.

The drives to the appointments were the most memorable for me. They gave me the perfect opportunity to discuss with Jarod things that were affecting his life, what Autism meant to him and his take on what was happening to him as a result.

It didn't take long to discover that because Jarod had been my only child with no early intervention to speak of, he had a lot less knowledge on the topic. Jarod had not thought a great deal about Autism even though we had discussed it many times in the previous two years.

Jarod was different to Ben, in that he chose to live largely in the moment. He didn't think too much about the consequences of his or others behaviour. Even when we discussed it, I could tell it wasn't 'going in'. Jarod was able to grasp the concept superficially, but on a deeper level he had difficulty and lost interest. Whenever I would bring up an example from his daily life, he'd think for a minute then say, "I don't know" and move on from the topic. For Jarod there was no motivation to work it out.

Jarod had many instances of social awkwardness in school. He was unable to work out whether kids were being nice to him, mucking around with him or teasing him. On the many occasions where he 'guessed' wrong, he found himself very confused and upset with himself and others.

Jarod tended to write people off. If another child teased him once, Jarod's hurt would cause him to view that child to be his enemy. He would no longer associate with them on any level. The people that he considered his friends were the kids that told him they will be his friend (nothing was assumed), do things for him and vice versa. For example, if someone was willing to lend Jarod money they were his friend. That is tangible, important and valuable to Jarod, therefore that value translates to the person who lent it. Friendships are based on loyalty, value, common interests and consistency.

Jarod learnt in class from the teachers that bullying and teasing are not nice things to do and shouldn't be tolerated. He, of course, took this literally, and as such if he experienced even a hint of teasing, he would write the person off as a bad person and a bully. I attempted on many occasions to talk to him about the subtle differences in teasing and fun behaviours and how some people may not intend to hurt him. Jarod always worried that if he forgave the person, then he may be 'asking for more'. For him shutting down would ensure he doesn't get hurt again. Opening up is a grey area, fraught with fears of being hurt or 'put down'.

Grey areas are uncomfortable for regular people but for people with Autism they can create huge gut aches. The unknown and unpredictable are incredibly scary.

#MikeyMonday
Mikey hugs me
Mikey: Mum I feel something weird
David: That's a rib Mikey.
Mikey: Oh yeah. Lucky you are still alive.

I met my husband Jason the night I turned eighteen. He was turning nineteen just three short days later. I remember the night clearly. He was wearing a 'save the seals' t-shirt and picked a flower from the garden to give me for my birthday. I liked him immediately. A friendship developed that night and three months later we became a couple. I admired his ability to cope with situations and the way in which he was so cool and calm with life. He was an intelligent man who had skills in many areas. I loved him deeply.

We were together for five years before we married and then another two years before Jarod was born.

Life as a newly married couple was blissful for me. We built our own home in our early twenties. My husband was attending University as a mature aged student when our first son Jarod was born. The blue-eyed smiley boy was the centre of both of our lives and we loved him deeply. Jarod would smile at anyone and everyone when he was a baby and he radiated the joy we felt at being first time parents. I enjoyed working and supporting our family while Jason studied.

As the years went by, our relationship had many opportunities to be strained. Obviously, the children's needs were significant, and our lives were incredibly stressful. We started to work together as a team rather than a couple and the concept of 'us' started to get lost. We both reacted differently to this. I blindly went forth taking care of the kids assuming our relationship would be there forever. I remained deeply in love with my husband and the signs of his unhappiness I unconsciously chose to ignore. The consequences of not being with him were absolutely terrifying.

Our great friendship slowly started to sour when he began to degrade me and disrespect me in public settings as well as at home. I started to live on tender hooks, 'hoping' that he would come home from work in a good mood. If he didn't, it affected the entire home and the kid's meltdowns were more frequent as a result.

One day out of instinct I picked up his phone. He had always been so protective of it. It was incredibly weird that he had gone for a shower and left it behind. I opened it. This small action changed my life forever. I found many, many messages, detailing the secret life he had been living with other women.

Immediately I was in the most pain I've have ever experienced in my life. I didn't confront him straight away as the kids were home. I didn't want to involve them in any arguments.

It would be days before I could even talk to him about what I knew.

The first day I spent making plans as to how I could end the relationship and make it the best possible experience I could for the kids. I arranged for a friend to take care of them while I packed up my husband's clothes. I texted him and told him it was over. He resisted briefly. He did not spend one more night in my home.

After, I picked up the kids and for a moment I watched their beautiful faces enjoy life as they knew it. Before I told them that things were never going to be the same. I told them daddy didn't love mummy anymore and that daddy was moving out. Mikey (largely nonverbal at the time) didn't understand and wandered off playing with toys.

The other three bawled with my sister and I there with them. I told them I loved them and that I would be there for them forever more. I told them they were the most important people in my life. I apologised for having changed their lives. I accepted responsibility for their dad leaving. I acknowledged that things were never going to be the same again and that that sucked for them.

Days later I looked my ex-husband square in the eye and asked the all-consuming question. The question I didn't really want to know the answer to. The one that would consume many of my hours and days to come. "Why?"

He laughed. It was a nervous kind of laughter, but laughter all the same. I couldn't stop the tears streaming then. It was like a tap had been released in my brain and the downpour was inevitable. I let the tears fall and kept my eyes on him. The silence ensued. The laughter faded. What was left was us. Just staring into each other's eyes. He spoke first. He took a deep breath and said, "It was fun. It was naughty and wrong, and I enjoyed it". My heart stopped. I couldn't believe I was here in this body, in this time, having this experience. I was so dumfounded by his honesty that I couldn't talk for the longest time.

Cheating was something that we'd often discussed as a clear 'no go' zone. My husband knew that by choosing this path, he was also choosing to end our relationship. I remember thinking how cowardly he had been up until that moment. He clearly wanted to end it but couldn't bring himself to do it. So, he forced my hand. Instead of a calm and reasonable separation, we got one born out of fire, anger, guilt, mistrust and regrets. For that I will always be grateful. I'm grateful because it was quick, it was clear and decisive.

I looked up at my ex-husband and told him that I would thank him one day for what he had done for me. I would appreciate the ease in which I was able to make the final decision to end our nineteen-year relationship. I knew it was the right choice. I could no longer live in a loveless marriage, where my husband professes his love to other women. I was abhorred and humiliated by his choices. But I was also freed. That day I took myself back and I became whole again. I began my relationship with myself and with my boys. We began our journey together, alone.

My husband and I talked for hours that day. We yelled. We were silent, and we ended 'us'. I mourned the relationship I thought I had. I had somehow invented it in my mind. My ex-husband told me he had mourned a long time ago in his mind. He had been treading water the last two years. He was genuinely surprised that I had been so shocked and heartbroken about it all. In his mind we were a couple 'living alone together'. In my mind we had been together forever.

The gut wrenching pain of being betrayed is like no other. I would gladly endure many more childbirths than repeat that experience. I was gutted to my very core and found the simple tasks in life, so hard to do.

My ex-husband and I never talked about getting back together. Neither of us entertained the idea at any point. My rage was all encompassing on that first day, but I knew that too would pass. I would never be looking back. I cried and cried the whole day, and when the kids came home I cried with them some more. I swallowed the rage when I looked into their innocent eyes and felt the immense guilt that I was the reason for their tears. I needed to be there for them. I'd done the worst thing that a child with Autism could want. I'd changed their entire world and I'd done so in the space of a day. I didn't take that lightly. I knew the best thing I could do was to give them everything I had when I was with them. Keeping as many things as possible the same, meant that my rage was going to be secondary to their needs.

I immediately told all my family and friends what had happened. I was overwhelmed with the most amazing support. I had professionals helping me with my mental health and finances. I had friends offering me meals, family members giving me money to help me to get by. I had so many offers of help for myself and for the kids.

The day after the separation, the boys and I all sat around the kitchen table having dinner. We chatted nicely, and the conversation flowed. I noticed that this kind of relaxed energy had not been present for years in the home and now it would be possible again. I knew that I had a hard road ahead of me, but I never once regretted my decision to raise the boys on my own from that time.

I saw how much love that was in my life. It just wasn't from my husband. I decided I needed to focus on love. Love was all around me. I was determined to tap into and experience all of it.

I looked at my four beautiful boys and I hugged them all ferociously. They were at the centre of my heart and soul. They were the reason I needed to move on. I needed to be strong. I needed to find the positive in those dire circumstances. I'd been practicing my positive affirmations and self- visualisations and I believed I could make something good come out of this.

For months afterward, every so often I would collapse into a chair, let out a deep breath and repeat the question, *Why?* to no one in particular.

When the answer never came, I got back up and trudged on.

It would be eight long years later that I would finally heal from this wound. Years and years of searching and attempting to 'forgive and move on' the final piece of the puzzle came quickly and easily in the end. I had spent so long feeling righteous in my 100% blame of my ex-husband for what had occurred, that I hadn't taken any responsibility for my part. Over the years my constant resentment and negative energy regarding him well and truly overtook the actions he had taken that lead to our separation. My bitterness toward him was unconsciously hurting me and the boys. Although I never outwardly spoke of him in a negative way, there was an unspoken thickness to the air when he was mentioned. One transformational weekend I took matters into my own hands and I called him out of the blue and apologised for my part in it all. This one call was all I needed to finally let go of the past and allow us all to move forward as a loving separated family. In a house full of love and acceptance there really was no place for grudges and drama that is best left in the past.

#MikeyMonday
Mikey finds a battery on the floor.
Mikey: Maybe this is a battery I can put my chest in.
Mikey puts it on his chest (where iron man has his one)
Mikey: I'm feeling a little overcharged.

When Ben was diagnosed and I began to read all those Autism books, I noticed how well my father seemed to 'fit' into this Autism Spectrum. For years our whole family knew some of my father's behaviours were 'odd' socially, but we always explained it away as 'Dad's Hungarian'. My reading showed a lot more insight into my father than it ever had before. I approached my mother with this information and she quickly agreed that my father has many Autistic tendencies.

I distinctly remember going on a drive with my father sometime after that and he said to me. "How are you going with Ben and the Autism?" I turned to dad and said, "If he turns out anything like you then I'll be proud as punch" and I meant it wholeheartedly. Dad smiled one of his awesome smiles and we continued the drive in silence. It was a profound moment for me, because as the words were coming out of my mouth I knew how true they were.

The qualities that made my dad different, quirky and 'Hungarian' also made him lovable, honest, open, committed and caring.

My dad had a very difficult childhood growing up during the Second World War. He saw a lot of death and suffering. He could easily have spent his adult years with anger 'hang-ups' and fears. Dad's Autistic qualities enabled him to put those experiences in the past where they belonged and enjoy a happy future. Truly enjoy it. Dad learned to appreciate what he had, and he modelled that to us as children.

Dad's ability to have an intense focus on one thing got him a job he enjoyed for years; working with computers. His passion for photography documented his children's lives. I am sure dad's Autism would have challenged my mum at times. His views on parenting, and his social awareness were somewhat left of centre, but Dad's love and energy would always shine through on us all.

My dad was our rock. I grew up in the suburbs of Melbourne with four siblings. Dad could always be relied upon to drive us to wherever we wanted to go. Even if that meant he would don a pair of roller skates with us at the local roller rink. It encouraged us to get out and experience the world.

As teenagers whenever we handed in a story about our father's life, we always received an 'A' for our efforts. Even now, thinking about his experiences I'm in awe at his emotional resilience and ability to 'move on' from things.

This might not seem so unusual for a father. The difference here is that my dad had been raised in war torn Hungary. He had many fascinating and challenging experiences during his formative years.

The following is an excerpt from his life story.

An episode my father is not likely to forget was when after a shopping trip, he and his father were walking back to a farm in Germany where they were staying. On their way back to the farm, they walked through several patches of tall pine-forests belonging to the adjoining farms.

At that time, near the end of the war, the Jewish prisoners were released by their German "Wehrmacht" soldier guards, but were still hunted down by some exuberant, armed SS officers. So most of the Jews begged the locals for some civilian clothes, to get rid of their grey & white striped prisoner uniforms. These patches of forests were the obvious places to change clothes. My father walked about ten metres in front of my grandfather, eager to get 'home, when he walked past one of those abandoned heaps of striped clothes - left by the trackside in the dimly lit forest. Suddenly the bundle moved and gave a spine-chilling snorting sound. He was a big Ukrainian Jewish man with a gaping bullet-hole on his forehead, still alive. He got onto his hands and knees trying to get up but was obviously beyond help. My father was terrified, and the sight burned a permanent picture in his memory.

At one point during the war in Hungary, my father's job was to take the trash to the local tip. He said there was a spot for the rubbish and a spot for the bodies. It was a commonly held belief, that soap was made from the fat from the dead and people bathed themselves in it.

My father's house was overtaken by German soldiers after my grandfather was taken as a prisoner of war. He was used to translate documents for them. The rest of the family were left to travel and wander on foot whilst their home was turned into a brothel by the maid. The stories and atrocities are endless.

Dad moved to Australia as a refugee at age of twenty-five. Brilliantly, my fathers 'Aspie' mind was able to put all his experiences in a file called 'the past' and let it all go. Growing up, the only ill effects I could see my father carried with him from his childhood was his reaction when he perceived we were wasting food. This reminded dad of the times in the war he was left begging for food.

That's it! That's all his 'hang ups'.

People are in therapy for a lifetime to learn to deal with things my father so easily compartmentalised. He remained in the present and created a happy life for himself. During my whole life, my dad has remained a positive, joyful and shining example of adjustability. I attribute all these abilities to his Autism (undiagnosed).

Seeing my dad succeed in life as he had done, helped me to perceive a positive future for my boys. More importantly, it got me thinking that this Autism thing might actually be an asset to one's life. This was a new idea for me. Beforehand it had been a condition to be managed and an unwanted disability.

#MikeyMonday
Mikey: You are mad at me.
Me: No, I'm not mad with you.
Mikey: Yes, you are, I can smell it.
Me: What does mad smell like?
Mikey: Like arm pit, it's gross, like dirt.

Ben became so aggressive one day. He grabbed Mikey by the neck and threatened that he had to be hurt. Jarod hurts him so Mikey was next in line. That logic didn't work on me. Surprise surprise.

I asked Ben to let Mikey go. I knew it was going to be big when this didn't happen for about thirty seconds. Ben pondered his anger vs. 'the right thing to do'. His anger subsided briefly enough to let Mikey go and Ben erupted. He slapped me in the face. He then said he felt that was the appropriate thing to do in this situation. My anger skyrocketed. He tried to go indoors to calm down but couldn't. I had to forcibly remove Ben outside and lock all the doors. He then took his anger out on the fence palings, outdoor chairs and the cubby house steps. The rage in his eyes was extreme. I let him take it out on the inanimate objects because I instinctively knew that this was the better option for that day. Some days I could avoid, some days it had to come out.

At dinnertime, I said to the other boys, "Ok now we pretend it didn't happen and we eat dinner". They accepted my lead and followed. When the meltdown had fully subsided a few hours later, I was able to talk to my Ben. The creature in the back yard from earlier was gone. He was able to articulate his anger. He understood the need to pay for the things he had broken.

I don't know if my way is the best way to handle a meltdown, but it's what works for me. I've spent many an occasion fighting with my kids about what they say and do during a meltdown. It just adds fuel to their fire, makes it last longer and become more intense. I find that rationalising with them doesn't happen during, only after. They are then able to talk about their feelings and actions. I switch into damage control mode. I make sure they aren't harming themselves or others. If they really need to, I let them go.

At first, I would worry I was letting them 'get away' with bad behaviour. Over the years, I know that I am raising some awesome kids. Kids who know right from wrong. Kids who sometimes have to let their balloons burst from time to time.

When I got to talk to the real Ben, we discussed healthy ways to let out anger. The next night, we were able to get out his breakable taekwondo board. We broke this over and over again, to get out the excess energy. Ben was happier with himself. His intelligence shone through to see that this is a better, smarter, option. But his motivation was to avoid having his pocket money used for three weeks, to pay for everything he broke. This was particularly hard, because money was Ben's special interest and I was messing with that.

I didn't get a complete win though. Ben would intermittently come up to me and tell me that I brought the meltdown on myself. He attempted to initiate a discussion about it. Engaging in that discussion would only lead to a repeat meltdown and was pointless. Ben accepted his punishment. That action speaks louder than any words can. It could not be about fault and blame.

#MikeyMonday
Kids are all watching TV
David: Is that the forty-two-year-old chick?
Mikey: It's a lunatic that's what it is Or a Luna-chick. Get it? Luna chick.

Jarod asked me one night, "Mum I need to talk about a few things that have had a significant impact on my life, can you tell me some?" I answered him in the matter of fact tone he enjoyed. "Maybe you could talk about your Autism or when dad and I separated?" He nodded and noted these things down. He was preparing for a talk he had to do at school.

Later, as he was doing his homework he asked, "Mum how has my Autism affected my life?". "Well it affects everything about your life, it affects the way you think, how you act, your social life…". He again nodded and methodically went about noting these things down, just like he was filling out a form.

At the time I smiled to myself. He'd taken a particularly emotionally challenging assignment and broken it down into easy to decipher facts and instances. My mind was both equally in awe and dumbfounded that such a serious topic, could be broken down so easily and detailed with little emotion. I was worried and proud at the same time. Two emotions that often coincided in my life.

A few days passed and then I happened to see his writing.

At first, I was perplexed trying to work out the context for the paper. Then the sadness followed. I was heartbroken for Jarod that he was in fact forced to endure a parental divorce. I was also sad that Jarod was able to remember seemingly insignificant details from the day that cemented it in his memory forever. He had processed it mechanically. It was really hard to be reminded of actions that I was responsible for, that affected my son's life in such a negative way.

Influences: The day I found out about my Autism, my parents divorced.

Script: The first influence of my life I'm going to talk about is my Autsim.

Autism is basically finding it hard to learn and do things socially. I remember the day I found out I had it. I told my mum about how I had had a really bad day at school, because everyone teased me. So, she decided to test me, I was positive. From that point on my life changed. I became slower to learn and became shyer in crowds. Although it is making it harder to do things like public speaking, I am slowly improving.

The second influence I want to talk about is my parents' divorce.

I remember in year seven when I came home from school. It was like any ordinary day. Then I saw one of my mum's friend's cars. Karen had picked me up from the bus stop because mum was too broken hearted to take care of us. We stayed at her house for tea, and then mum picked us up later. When she came we found out why we stayed at Karen's house. Dad had left mum. She took us home and told us the full story. Out of the blue, dad went to her and said "I can't do this anymore. I'm sorry. But I just want us to be friends". This has had a major impact on my life because I learnt that not everyone's lives are good. Also, the change of only seeing my dad once every fortnight and swapping houses every fortnight has not made my life easy.

Experiences can change a person's life forever, these things, although they happened years ago, are still having an on effect on my life today. My Autism is making it harder to speak in public and use common sense. The divorce is making me worried about trying new things.

Mikey: Mum it's time to take me to school.
Me: But there was a cute guy on a video I had to watch.
Mikey: What's happening to you mum? You are acting more like a teenager.
He might have a point there I guess!

I've had many gut wrenching moments in my life. I'm sure most would not envy. I have found myself having to re-live childhood memories of being teased and 'left out' socially when my children went through similar experiences.

Sometimes I wanted to go through my days with blinders on. Taking the kids at face value and not talking to them about what's underneath. That way, I can almost believe their whole lives are fantastic. Other times, I know I need to scratch under the surface and get to the root of the issue, so I can help them to function better.

I had planned a sleepover birthday party for David who was turning nine. Usually when I did this, I tried to arrange for some of the other kids to have sleepovers at others houses to avoid clashes.

I didn't do that this time, because I had wrongly assumed that a nine-year-old would pose no interest to my older boys. This was true enough for Jarod, who spent the weekend in his bedroom with his Xbox. His only issue was when I asked him to give up his game controller, aka his left arm, for the partygoers.

Ben on the other hand struggled terribly with the combination and 'pecking order' in the house. Ben fancied himself a controller of the group and wanted to run the games with his own rules. He didn't want to give up his controller and wanted to spend all his time with them.

After a short period of time David approached me and asked if Ben could play somewhere else. To say Ben was offended by this was an understatement. Ben couldn't perceive himself to be a hindrance to a situation. Even if he could, he absolutely didn't want to. The meltdown started way before I was able to reach him with logic. Like so often, I found myself putting out 'spot fires' with him while trying to run a fun party for David and his friends.

Ben's meltdowns tended to involve everyone around him. He said some pretty mean things during them. He said he would have preferred to go to a friend's house, so out of desperation I arranged for that to occur. I went into Ben's room to tell him the good news, but I was met with an even bigger meltdown. He didn't want to go. He was afraid his friend would see him 'like this' and he'd say something bad to his friend. Although an admirable quality in a friend, this meant I would need to bear the brunt of the meltdown and take care of eight other kids.

Ben burst into tears and rocked himself for a while. He eventually went to sleep. The whole weekend was filled with rocky waters. By Sunday night we were all exhausted. Ben came out to talk to me Sunday night and I knew I could ignore it no longer. If I didn't deal with what's behind the emotional outbursts, they would become more frequent and more violent.

I invited Ben to come and sit on my lap. He often told me he is in the one percent of kids his age that are still happy to hug their mothers. I loved it. Ben started off by telling me his head felt wrong and he was having trouble sleeping. I suggested that his behaviour this weekend was perhaps making him feel a little guilty because of his treatment of others.

He agreed with this as he often did post meltdown and was filled with remorse about his actions. This conversation is one we shared many times both by choice and by necessity. The territory was familiar at first.

We talked about Autism, and its effect on Ben's life, at length. He talked about having a meltdown and crying in class, because he accidentally wore his sports shoes to high school. He had been mortified. Not because he was in any sort of trouble, but just that it was 'wrong' and he found it hard to function knowing that. Ben told me he sometimes woke up on a school morning thinking, 'I can't get through this'. He said he never looks forward to it because it can be so overwhelming. All it took was one small thing to make him snap. As Ben talked more my heart broke for him again.

By carefully structuring his world I enabled him to cope with his life. I didn't take on board the significance of the Autism and the natural struggles that go along with it. I made the mistake of focusing on surface issues. Mostly because I knew delving deeper would involve more heartache as it would be hard to acknowledge. Especially hard because most of it involves things I can't 'fix'. I didn't want to be too hard on myself either though.

I didn't usually do denial for long. With Autism you can't ignore issues. They get bigger and then the meltdowns dictate the outcome.

The false sense of security of smooth sailing makes you doubt yourself when something does happen. *Maybe I should have foreseen this? Maybe I should have dealt with it sooner? Maybe I'm just doing the best I can with the cards I've been dealt? Maybe I have a very complex hand?* Questions that have no real answer. The grey in-between is confusing and at times soul crushing. No rights or wrongs. Just choice.

#MikeyMonday
Mikey: I love you mum.
Me: I love you too.
Mikey: Thanks for helping us.
Me: You know it's my job to make you feel better in your life
We enjoy a cuddle.
Mikey: What's that smell?
Me: Probably my breath.
Mikey: Eww
Special moment = over!

I was enjoying my kid free weekend with a spot of shopping. I was in the city, which meant I could go to my favourite shop - the Converse factory outlet. Since I was a young child, I always had a liking for all shoes Converse. When I was a teenager, of course, that meant red high tops, but now they come in all colours and styles.

Wading through them, I was in heaven. I tried on about ten pairs of sneakers whilst procrastinating incessantly and changing my mind as many times. I stumbled across a pair of black and white high tops with the Joker's face imprinted on them. It would probably be prudent now to mention, that my eldest son Jarod had a huge passion for all things Batman.

My mind swirled. I could see the light in his eyes as he wore these sneakers and the lights in mine when I saw him finally wearing 'less nerdy' footwear. I ummed and ahhhed for a while, but in the end, I rationalised that it was a factory outlet and therefore much cheaper than retail. The kids never get good shoes, so it would be ok if they all got a pair just this once.

My head was swarming, and I was loving every minute of it. A sales assistant quickly realised I might need some help as I was walking around the shop with four boxes in my arms. Thankfully she helped me work out the best shoes for each one of the kids. Similar styles for the little ones, so they all felt a fair process had occurred. I was on a massive shopping high when I walked out of the shop with my huge box full of goodies.

My kids arrived, and I didn't waste any time telling them I had surprises for them. My kids, looking perplexed, peered into the car and saw the boxes. And that's when it happened. It's what I affectionately refer to as an 'Aspie reaction' ensued.

Jarod took one look at the Joker sneakers and said he didn't like them. After all, the Joker was Batman's arch enemy. As if that wasn't enough, he went on to say that he didn't need sneakers anyway and asked me why I would get him any at all. Mikey had trouble putting his on and threw them away saying they were stupid. Ben said he thought his were ok, but he'd prefer high tops.

My heart sank. I said as much to the kids and then reluctantly offered to go back to the shop to change them over. After all, I wasn't spending all that money on shoes that weren't going to get worn!

On the way to the shop David who hadn't uttered a word since he got his shoes says, 'I might look in the shop too to see if I want to change mine'. It was then that I lost it. I'm not sure how long I ranted, but it was at least a few minutes. I reminded the boys that I was doing this out of the kindness of my heart and their reaction was both rude and hurtful.

By the time we got to the shop Ben was feeling sick in the stomach about his role in the whole thing. We entered the shop and greeted the less enthusiastic sales assistant again. The boys spent very little time selecting shoes they preferred and after paying more for the shoes, than I had originally, we were able to leave again. I was feeling a bit better that the younger boys had agreed to keep their original purchase and we only had to exchange two pairs. Not surprisingly Jarod chose a pair of Batman sneakers with no Joker in sight. He was definitely keen on staying on the 'good side' of that franchise.

As we were leaving the shop, I said to Jarod "Are you happy with these ones?"

"Yeah they are ok, but I still don't get why I'm getting them, when I don't need sneakers."

It was then that it fell into place. I immediately chastised myself for the whole encounter. It was me who set up the situation. I bought shoes they hadn't asked for, didn't really need and weren't expecting. Then I had the audacity to expect a favourable response to the whole thing. I cursed myself for not texting my ex-husband and asking him to warn the children they were getting a gift they needed to appreciate. I cursed myself for not realising the Joker was a 'baddy' and as such would be frowned upon. I cursed myself for projecting my love of all things Converse onto the kids, assuming they would have similar affections. I knew all of the above beforehand, they just didn't occur to me at the time.

With these thoughts my calm nature returned. I reminded the kids that although I understood their reactions, they weren't going to impress a future wife with that kind of brutal honesty in the face of a gift.

At the end of my monologue, Jarod said to me "So I guess you have learned a lesson here then." I agreed that indeed I had and asked him if he could say the same. His delayed answer of "I suppose I have" spoke volumes. I suspected that what he had learned was in fact not the lesson I had been trying to convey. I was exhausted from the day's activities and chose to let it go, rather than be disappointed all over again by his response.

Mikey comes into my room first thing in the morning
after having a head cold for a couple of days.
Me: Here's my sickie. How are you feeling?
Mikey: Just a second. I need to puke in the toilet.

I've had heaps of hearty discussions with many different people about my kids having the label of Autism. Many fear that having the label may in fact, make life harder for my kids.

When Ben was diagnosed with Autism the decision to share this with others was not taken lightly. It had occurred to me that we could keep this information 'in house'. I thought that maybe Ben might grow to consider it a private thing. I worried what others might think and how they might treat him if they knew.

Anyone who knows me well, knows that even if I were to try to do this, it wouldn't have lasted long. I have a bit of a 'tell all' attitude when it comes to my life. I really didn't see a reason this would be any different.

In the end I chose the full disclosure approach. We told everyone in our lives. We even sent letters home to the Kindergarten parents when he started there, so that people would be aware that there is a reason, other than misbehaviour, for Ben's eccentricities.

This approach turned out to be extremely successful. I had complete strangers approaching me offering their words of encouragement and support. Parents were understanding of Ben's behaviours. They explained his brain differences with their kids whenever there was an issue. They said that his brain works slower in some areas and faster in others. He is wired differently.

As Ben got older, he joined us in talking about his diagnosis openly with his friends and schoolmates. It was never an issue at all. I think this was because armed with the knowledge; parents were able to approach Ben differently. They saw his behaviours as indicative of a condition, rather than seeing him as naughty, rude, or weird. I was a little surprised when this happened. I feared that some parents might not like having a 'different' child playing with theirs. My own childhood memories of being teased for being 'a nerd' resurfaced. Thankfully these fears were quickly squashed, as parents responded with overwhelming support.

Jarod, who was diagnosed with Autism at age ten, chose the more conservative approach. Friends and family knew about the diagnosis, but the wider circle of people in our lives were not told. Jarod had many issues with friends in primary school and was worried this news would make it even harder for him in the playground.

Ben was once approached by a boy on the school bus and was teased. He was called "ass-burgers" repeatedly. Ben's response was to ask the boy incredulously, "Why would you make fun of my disability?" The boy didn't stop, and many insults were thrown back and forth both ways. Ben was joined by two friends that supported and stood up for him. The other boy was alone.

Jarod, upon hearing what had happened on the bus, which he was present on, and blissfully unaware of anything (courtesy of his iPhone music) says to Ben "See this is what you get for telling people about Autism".

I asked Ben how he felt about people knowing. His immediate response was "I'm proud of the Autism (also formerly known as Asperger's Syndrome) mum."

I have often wondered that if Jarod was diagnosed earlier whether I would have automatically told others and elicited the support that

Ben received. This may have then circumvented some of his social issues that led to the request for secrecy?

Others not knowing might have not given kids the ammunition to use their disability as a focus for teasing. I was led to wonder if this secrecy was in fact more desirable for teenagers affected by Autism. The events of this have gone around in my head many times. I keep coming back to the math. For every kid there is who is willing to tease Ben and kids like him, there are two others willing to 'stick up' for him. That speaks volumes to me.

Later, Jarod too would become proud of his diagnosis. He has been known to heartily laugh when his friends jokingly refer to the condition. Now all my boys wear their diagnosis with a sense of pride and achievement, for the gift it brings to their lives.

#MikeyMonday
Me: I can't believe they are taking so long in the
drive thru, we only ordered drinks.
Mikey: Relax mum you've got me here, it's all G.
Me: Yes, that's true Mikey, it's all G (good) when I have you here.

We have always taken things very literally in our house. When I would say "I'll be there in a minute", I was. I would never tell my kids to take their time or to do something when they are ready. If I say, "hop on over there and pick that up for me", I had better expect to see some actual hopping occur.

An extensively planned family holiday to Fiji, involved a big social story with every movement outlined in precise detail. I knew when I left that Mikey in particular, would need to have as much information as possible to feel comfortable in a new environment. For the most part he was. What I didn't plan on was the social niceties biting me.

A few days in, we all decided to take the local village tour. The elders of the village talked about Fijian culture and history of course including their well-known cannibalistic component. The man finished his speech off by joking that you need to always say "Bula" when a Fijian does, otherwise they might eat you. Everyone laughed. Mikey freaked! The other boys and I all explained to Mikey that the man had been only joking and he seemed to be ok with this for a bit.

Four days later, I noted that the usually socially shy Mikey was approaching total strangers saying "Bula" many times a day. It did occur to me that he had taken the tour guide literally, but I didn't think it was doing much harm. In fact, it had brought out the social side of him.

What I didn't plan on was for a local to yell 'Bula' from the side of the road while we were driving. Mikey's rush to return the greeting fell short of the man's ears and he saw it. Before I knew it, Mikey was hitting himself in the head and repeating, "He's going to eat me", "Oh no, I get eaten", over and over again. I had to give Mikey the biggest bear hug and reassure him that no one was getting to eat my boy ever! He had obviously not believed the man was joking. Instead of trying this tact again, I said I would always protect him from anyone who would try to hurt him. That, he found easier to believe.

Jarod was telling us all about how he was required
to dance at school for an experiment.
Jarod: I wished I were dead
Mikey: Me too cause then I can get your Xbox One.

One weekend, I was invited to a dress up engagement party. I prepared the kids that I was going out and that we would be wearing zombie make up for the theme of the party. A friend came over and spent a great deal of time covering me from head to toe in grey and white, then added the black and of course the 'blood' came last. I looked fantastic! Or so I thought.

I had been showing the kids the progress all along, but unfortunately the final product was too much for poor ten-year-old David. He took one look at me and bawled his eyes out. The look of sheer terror in his face hit me hard. He immediately covered himself in a blanket, dropped into a foetal position and started rocking back and forth. For the first time in my mothering life I found myself in the position of not being able to comfort my own child. I was the reason he was crying.

Thankfully in our family, I have many children and a range of phobias. Jarod had shared a fear of zombies when he was younger. I quickly enlisted his help to comfort David from 'scary mum'. I then disappeared to the party. Through messaging I learnt that David had in fact calmed down. Jarod was able to be perfectly empathetic of David because he had experienced the same fear and understood it.

David told me the next day that when he saw me, he thought that I had turned into a zombie. In his mind, he was unable to reconcile the difference between a dress up and reality.

I have experienced this often with my kids and their imagination. Often people believe that Autistic kids don't have an imagination. I think this is a simplistic explanation. Rather my kids seem to take their imaginations into overload and somehow get mixed up between the real and the imaginary. For David, mum was really a zombie that night and when the makeup was off the next day, she wasn't.

David was talking about how muddy he got at school.
Mikey: My schools special. There is no mud.
That's why it's called a special school.

As a young toddler Mikey would enjoy eating charred pieces of wood from our fire place, Blu-Tak, sand in huge crunching mouthfuls and Play Dough. His absolute favourite thing to eat though was a thick kids book. He would wander around for hours carrying his latest book, scraping his teeth on it and eventually devouring the whole thing.

Although none of these things seemed to cause Mikey any permanent damage it would be a huge stretch for me to say it didn't cause me some stress as a mother.

I was on a bit of a roller coaster with his foods after that.

It was very clear to me, very early on; Mikey would eat only the foods he wanted to eat. He was non-verbal for many years, he didn't speak at all, so I couldn't be sure why some foods were ok and others not so much. Mikey communicated by grabbing my hand and dragging me to the item he wanted. Or he would simply yell and scream, and I was required to guess what he wanted.

I knew that texture; colour, smell, temperature and looks were key factors. Whenever we would try something we thought would fit the bill, it was often met with outright rejection. After many years of encouraging, cajoling, recommending, educating, disciplining and even trying to put the food in his mouth myself, I had decided another method was in order. I would present his tea every night and if he ate it, all well and good, but if he didn't that was ok too. I would make sure to put veggies on Mikey's plate every night and every night he would leave them there.

After two years of this technique I struck gold. Mikey decided that he would make himself a taco with minced meat and grated carrot. I had to try to contain my excitement at dinner so as not to 'spook' him, but needless to say I was jumping up and down in my head!

Try and try again I would, but years later grated carrot was still the one and only vegetable Mikey would eat voluntarily and only on tacos.

I'm filling you in on all this background for a reason. I want you to understand my lie. Raising kids of any description, most parents would agree that honesty is a quality we wish to instil in our children.

Raising kids on the Autism Spectrum it becomes a necessity. My kids thrive on my complete honesty with them. Lies are confusing and frustrating for them. They find it extremely difficult to tell them, as well as understand their purpose. My kids catching me in a lie has led to many meltdowns in my house. There has to be absolute honesty and reliability in their mother, so they have a point of reference with which to view the world. If they can't trust me, they will have trouble trusting anyone.

One day I came home with half a cow to put in my freezer. Mikey saw the mince and became really distressed that it came from a cow. I made his favourite tacos for dinner that night and he refused to eat them. His brothers and I repeatedly explained to Mikey that the meat was the same as it always had been. But the thought of it being a cow was too much for him to bear. Mikey cried and ran to his room barely eating anything at all.

You can imagine my disappointment that the only vegetable Mikey ate was now off the list.

So, you can probably guess what I did the next night? Yep that's right! I sat Mikey down and told him I had made the leftover tacos the old way, not from a cow and he ate every bite. I then proceeded to tell all the other children, that if they told Mikey the truth they would be in big trouble!

#MikeyMonday
Me: Mikey why didn't you want to visit your new baby cousin?
Mikey: Because babies are gross. They come from
mummy's tummies through the vagina.

I guess for the most part, being in an area of 'grey' makes my boys feel like something is wrong. "I'm not sure", is something I rarely hear come out of their mouths. Even if they aren't sure, my kids will usually make an assumption based on the information at hand, rather than stay in the 'middle'.

I can only assume from my experience that this is due to the sensory challenges of Autism. My children have often described it that they tend to focus on one thing at a time, e.g. seeing and hearing can come one after the other and do not seem to occur simultaneously. For that reason, the world can seem very overwhelming with so many external and internal stimuli for them to process and deal with.

When Mikey was twelve, he was told by one of his brothers, that a friend of the family that was his age was his girlfriend. As a child who could barely tolerate having one friend and three brothers in his life, this information really scared him. As a result, almost two years later, he still rarely spoke to any girls. If asked an innocent question, like who is the girl that catches the taxi with him, he wouldn't even tell me her name.

I've often pondered why Mikey felt he needed to make such seemingly extreme decisions. I guess to him they aren't so extreme.

The idea of having a girlfriend scared him. He's not sure how one obtains a girlfriend. Or what's involved in the process, other than the need for a girl in the equation. So, he did what he could do to avoid it all. No girl = no problem.

For Jarod at age sixteen, if the wheelbarrow is out of action, he then he assumes can't go get any wood for the fireplace. His logic would tell us we need to be cold rather than find another way to bring the wood in.

Early in his life, Ben realised he really disliked the taste of chocolate. He obviously chose from then on not to eat any. The only problem was he discovered that there were many foods that were 'chocolate flavoured' and he didn't want to take the risk that they could be. So Ben made an all or nothing choice. He decided to eat nothing that was the colour brown at all. This was the only way felt he could be sure to avoid tasting chocolate. He stuck to this course for over ten years.

When David was ten, if he saw or heard something that scared him, he struggled to get it out of his mind. Watching a documentary, he saw a fake human eye being hurt. He immediately felt the pain as if it was his own eye, as we all did for a second. Hours later he couldn't get the image out of his mind. He couldn't sleep. He couldn't close his eyes at all without seeing it all over again. I spent two hours very late at night cuddling and cajoling him to think happier thoughts. He rocked, he shook and he cried uncontrollably until eventually, he was so exhausted he fell asleep on the couch while I sat in the chair opposite. The next day, the image was gone, and he went happily to school.

The ability to see and experience life in its extremes can be somewhat debilitating, as in Mikey and David's examples. I've also witnessed it to be very freeing for my kids. They have felt good when they have learnt to control the world around them in their own special way. They have found their own way around their issues, using things that work for them. I can imagine that's why Autistic people are said to be brilliant inventors. They can see solutions to problems that others, who don't have the need to shut out all the overwhelming data they are presented with, don't need to see.

#MikeyMonday
Mikey: What's the weather today?
Ben: About 20.
Mikey: 20% sunny?
Ben: No, 20 degrees
Mikey: Oh. I asked for the weather but ok
Ben: ?

I like to describe myself as an avid reader. Mostly I tend to seek out fun, happy, easy reading books that interest me and don't tear at my heartstrings too much. I have often been recommended to read books about Autism and always asked, how will it make me feel?

As I mentioned earlier, I actively chose to avoid stories that will sadden and depress me. I have found it hard to give my children the attention they need when I have that mindset.

I discovered the world of Autism on Facebook in about 2012. I was reading and 'liking' a whole bunch of Autism pages and updates. After a few months of this, I actually realised that I have always avoided a certain 'perspective'. That perspective is very simple, it is the 'glass is half empty' theme.

When you avoid reading books like that it's harder to notice how others see the world. The beauty and downfall of Facebook, is that different perspectives are all there at a glance. Many talk about the lack of support and understanding they receive from friends, family members and the general community. It has often irked me that people will openly complain about not getting help from others.

If people without kids offer advice on how to help your kids it is often seen as an insult. I've always thought that maybe they are just trying to empathise with you and help you? I always tried to look at the intention and energy behind the words rather than the words themselves.

What I find interesting is determining if this is their 'regular mindset' or if they were simply having a bad day?

I had a particularly difficult 'Mother's Day' one year. My first instinct was to keep it to myself and not share my 'depressed state' with the world. As I've said, I'm a big believer in what you focus on expands so I was reluctant to give attention to this experience.

As with most things, upon reflection and more thought, I realised that again this comes back to perspective. I had a really hard day. My expectation, and hope that things would be different, was my downfall.

I'm embarrassed to admit that I unconsciously hoped the day would revolve around me. Now I know intellectually that in Autism-land that is not likely. Especially without significant prompting, social stories and motivation in the form of rewards. But for some reason my emotional being wanted more. The day was just like any other day. No gifts, no cards, no acknowledgement at all of the role I had played in their life.

I wallowed in the 'have not's rather than enjoying the 'haves'. I didn't look at the intention of my boys. I focused on the words and actions. I wanted them to be 'different' for the day. My boys love and cherish me in their own special way and that has always been their intention. From their perspective, lavishing me with compliments and performing loving tasks was unnecessary. They believed I knew how they felt about me, so there was no need to make a fuss about it.

The positive I chose to see in expressing these feelings, is that I was able to see where I don't want to be. I chose a different perspective - about my children, Autism, the world and the people in it. The negative and the positive both serve a purpose. The glass is half empty perspective for me is exhausting, depressing and inhibits my ability to function in the world.

Just allowing myself to remain in that space for one day, took me five days to recover. I know, by experiencing the contrast, that I chose the right path for my family and me.

Mikey at age twelve said to me "Mum, when you die I'm going to hug you forever". Now that's what I'm going to focus on!!

#MikeyMonday

Mikey and David have an appointment at the dentist.

Dentist: So, you guys got the day off school to come to the dentist.

David: Yeah.

Mikey: Day off indeed.

Dentist smiles

Me: You are an old man aren't you gorgeous.

Mikey: I'm not an old man and yes.

Answered both questions nicely there

As I mentioned earlier, Jarod's early development took a somewhat similar path to typical kids. He spoke, he walked, he interacted and he was no trouble to raise. His younger brothers were delayed; they were in need of strict routines and were prone to loud ongoing meltdowns when asked to perform simple tasks. It wasn't until he was in grade three and four that we began to notice he wasn't developing quite like his peers.

Jarod had always been a literal and visual learner. He always spoke with unusual tones and inflection. The words he chose would be 'adult like' in nature. I had thought of these as 'cute quirks' about Jarod, not 'Autistic symptoms'. Jarod didn't seem to have the classic overload button I was so used to seeing. Jarod always had these symptoms but he was just better at hiding them.

Jarod, being very intelligent learned to mimic facial expressions at a young age. He realised a certain 'look' from me meant stop what you are doing and look 'regretful and forlorn'. It took me years to realise that he did not actually understand what behaviour I might have been disappointed with. He just knew one look required a certain one reciprocated on his face. I was often frustrated when he would repeat a behaviour I had just scolded him for, assuming he was being naughty. He knew the face to make, but not the reason why.

His meltdowns are now often termed 'shutdowns'. If he was overwhelmed with something or not happy with how things were going, he would lie down silently and just stay there. At the time I assumed it was just a tantrum he was having. I would step over him and leave him alone to 'get over it'. This technique worked. It was not because I was accurately assessing the situation, but because he was able to have time alone to calm down and process his feelings.

All my kids have given me fantastic life lessons but in this one Jarod had given me the gift of non- assumption, if there is such a thing. I no longer assume my kids, or anyone for that matter knows what I'm thinking or feeling just by my facial expression or even my words.

I ask them to relay what they know about what I mean, to make sure we are on the same page. I try not to berate myself for 'reading a whole different book', where Jarod was concerned in his early years. We both get each other now and that's what matters.

#MikeyMonday

Mikey: I'm going to keep this for the next year in a container.

Me: What is it?

Mikey: It's a joint name.

Jarod: you mean your name in cursive?

Mikey: Um, yeah.

When I drove the kids to school each day I usually discussed what they are doing at school that day etc. On one of these journeys I was floored with a dilemma I wasn't expecting. Mikey, as per usual, was talking about how he had cooking one day, then community access the next, followed by swimming and a camp. David sighed and said, "I wish I went to Mikey's school, it's so much more fun than ours". He meant it; he really wished that was his school.

My initial response was to sprout the rhetoric I had heard as a child many times. "These kids don't have anywhere near the opportunities you guys will have in the future". The sub-context of this being, "They might as well have fun now because they aren't capable of much else". We feel sorry for them so we make up for it, by giving them fun things to do. My generation taught me that kids who go to a specialist school, won't amount to much. I was saddened that this was in fact still the case in larger society as had been in my eyes a few short years earlier.

I wanted to break this out dated pattern of thinking, but I wasn't sure how. I wasn't sure what to say. That day, I ended up taking the easy option most of us mothers do of not answering at all. I just did my usual drop offs as if nothing had been said. This may seem cowardly, but I really needed to ponder this one. I was heartened that the children I was raising did not share societies judgments about belittling and pitying those that attended specialist schools. But I was also annoyed with myself that I couldn't easily find words to counter what the kids had said immediately. That meant for me that I must still have residual issues about this topic.

Years ago, I had thought Mikey's education would be a struggle. I twisted my mind and stomach in knots trying to work out what would be best for his future development and wellbeing. Mikey had received all the group and individual therapy I could organise and spent a blissful year in kindergarten with kid's who have regular needs.

It was actually one of the hardest decisions I have ever had to make, sending Mikey to a specialist school. The decision was inevitable but weighed on me nevertheless. It was so agonising as I was forced to revaluate my pre-held beliefs that kids who went to special school and their families, were to be waved to and not spoken about. We were never encouraged to make friends with kids with special needs. Instead I was taught to 'leave them alone' and pity them. It was also brutal for my senses because that meant my child had a severe disability. What comes with a severe disability? A lifelong commitment to their care. That idea was so scary I would not let myself think about it for many years. I just took each day as it came and learned to live life in the present moment.

The following is a snapshot of what life was like for Mikey at Kinder. It's is an excerpt of one of Mikey's kinder newsletters addressing the parents about him...

> A highlight this year was having Mikey in our class. The children and staff have learnt so much from him about acceptance and the knowledge that everyone has strengths and weaknesses – with practice we can do anything.
>
> This year the children have been very understanding when Mikey has tried to communicate, which comes out

more like a scream. With help they understood he couldn't ask to borrow toys and so he would just take them.

This was very daunting for the kinder children; twenty-one other children Mikey needed to share with and understand what they wanted – a huge challenge for him. As the year has gone on we have seen Mikey learn to share, wait and go to the toilet like a big kinder boy. He has learnt the kinder routine and been able to independently go from one transition to the next. He has mastered every puzzle in our cupboard and we have well over a hundred! He has designed many different railway tracks and learnt to share his precious trains with friends.

One day we saw some of the children who were struggling with Mikey's unpredictable behaviour, start to relax and work with him. Rather than come to a teacher we saw them use the tools we had given them as saying 'wait' taking their train back and giving Mikey a spare one to play with. We also saw Mikey accept direction from his new kinder friends.

The children learnt to use the picture cards around the room and we would often find the children holding the cards right in front of his nose repeating the word waiting for him to say it back to them. They were disappointed when he didn't and for about two terms we heard "Is he ever going to talk?"

Third term; another student learnt that when she pulled him on the go-cart and stopped he would say "more". A word from Mikey to communicate with his peers – what a breakthrough. Mikey wrote M on his artwork.

Fourth term – Mikey came to kinder and said the teacher's names. My heart stopped and tears welled. He then repeated each of the children's names at the table I was sitting at. He copied words I had written down.

Last week at mat time Mikey sat with me saying the children's names, repeating them after I said them. When children gave him a toy he said thank you. If they took a toy he said "No, no no". The children certainly noticed the changes and they have all been working with him to say THEIR name.

My last newsletter for 2007. Each year I try to teach diversity, a comfort with different nationalities, abilities, genders and people. It is very hard for children to feel comfortable with 'difference' unless they live it, practice it and with time 'different becomes normal'. I think Mikey has taught us more this year about acceptance than I could ever have manufactured with dolls, books or pictures. Narelle Kolody

Mikey enjoyed the support of wonderful staff and students at our local Kinder. For a long time, I wished he could stay there wrapped in a warm cocoon of acceptance.

#MikeyMonday
As we were leaving the Christmas party for kids with special needs.
David: I've still got Batman on my face.
Me: It's ok I've still got glitter in my hair!
Mikey: I haven't got anything on me.... except
the smile on my face I can't wipe off.

I wrote the following after Mikey's first transition visit to the specialist school...

Mikey's kinder year ended with mixed emotions for me. I was so happy with all the progress he'd made and yet I knew we couldn't stay in this warm, welcoming kinder bubble forever. Mikey would need to spend time in the world with bigger kids, learning new things in a place with less familiarity and new rules.

With a heavy heart I decided that the only safe place for Mikey to go to school would be somewhere fenced. Somewhere people were specially trained to deal with his behaviours and needs. Somewhere the staff ratio would mean he would get the time and attention he needs. Somewhere he could associate with kids at his cognitive level and social ability. A specialist school.

The sun was shining so brightly you would have thought nothing could upset me that day. I'd had years to get used to the behaviours, the diagnosis, the explanations to friends and family and the grief. But of course, it all came back, not as bad, and for not as long, but it was back. I took one look at the school where my son 'belonged' and I wanted to cry.

There were huge locked gates surrounding the classrooms and play areas. A necessity in a school like this one and my child needed it too. I reminded myself it was one of the reasons I chose this school.

I wanted to take my child, walk through the gate and run the other way screaming. Instead, I was directed to the classroom where my child would be spending most of his time. The locked door was opened and we were inside.

Mikey sat on my lap with his hands over his ears. We watched five children in five different directions, engaged in various activities. The noise level was extreme. Mikey and I were both very aware of it. I wanted to cover my ears too. After a few minutes Mikey was happy to leave my arms for few moments. He ran straight to a Thomas the Tank Engine book. He loved Thomas. It was that book that enabled him to explore the room more fully. The book somehow gave him the security to roam the room and see what he could touch. He carried the book under his arm through the whole visit and was very reluctant to give it back when it came time to go.

I was more than ready to get out of there. It was hard to watch the teachers and assistants with these severely disabled children, trying to teach them to read, feed themselves, walk, and stick things to paper. I wondered how we got to this. Why my son needed to learn in this environment with these kids. The answer of course was simple. He was one of them. He was as disabled as them. This fact hit hard while I was there.

I made a snap decision, the briefest of mistakes and I was going to pay for that for some time ahead. It was because of my haste to leave the school. My heightened emotion, that led me to not think properly. I told Mikey that he would need to leave his beloved new Thomas book at the School where it belonged. The teacher, not realising what was to follow, supported my decision and attempted to take the book from him. That is when the screaming started. A full-blown meltdown, in the middle of the jail we had chosen to lock ourselves in.

My worst nightmare was coming true. *I should have seen the signs, I could have avoided this*, was all I thought. But of course, it was too late. I knew I had paid for my ticket on the rollercoaster years ago, so now I needed to go through the loops and hold on as best I could.

I decided after a few short minutes that there would be no way he would come to the car of his own accord. I physically grabbed him, put him on my hip and proceeded to walk swiftly to the car. I tried hard to maintain my external persona of 'managing' these situations calmly. The school staff were very experienced and they knew all too well what I was going through. It was their understanding eyes that almost sent me to tears.

I can't cry now. I just need to get him into the car and then we'll be fine I thought. He pulled my hair, kicked me and punched me all the way to the car. The staff followed quietly but supportively. In the car it took another five minutes to put him into his seat and do up the seat belt. Fortunately, I'd had the foresight to purchase a special car seat that fitted bigger children with a five- point harness, for occasions such as this. He couldn't get this seat belt off so was safer for him. I was saddened by the knowledge that this was the best place for him to be. Strapped in a car seat he couldn't get out of. He could, however, calm down in his car seat without hurting himself or others around him.

The staff apologised many times for not foreseeing the event, but I knew that it was me that had made the wrong decision. The decision that most five-year old's would have little difficulty with understanding and accepting. I should have known that this book was the glue keeping him together and functioning in this new unfamiliar place. I tore it off him, and left him feeling alone, scared and vulnerable.

I said a hasty goodbye to the staff and was relieved when we pulled out of the parking lot. I would let myself cry then, now I was alone. Unfortunately, today was not the day that the screaming would stop in the car. Mikey flailed and screamed all the way home. It is usually a fifteen-minute drive to my small hometown, but that day it would take me forty-five minutes.

I was forced to pull over several times while Mikey pulled my hair, screamed and kicked at everything he could reach. He was out of control and I nearly was too. All I could do was cuddle him and tell him everything was o.k. Something I wasn't sure if he understood or was at all comforted by. He didn't speak so I didn't really have any idea what he understood even though I talked to him often. But it was what I needed to do. For me.

When I got home, I was both comforted and concerned to realise that it was Tuesday. Girls Lunch. A huge group of ladies with their kids, were at my house for the weekly luncheon. This was usually an acceptable experience for Mikey, but today was different. I dried my tears and took a deep breath as I walked into the house. More screaming. It was no use pretending. I burst into tears right there and was immediately comforted by several of my friends. 'I am so lucky', was my thought 'to have such wonderful and caring friends'. It is their positive presence that keeps me going.

I took Mikey to the television and put on his favourite video. I made him a 'bot bot' and sat impatiently with him waiting for composure to return. Fortunately, the calm descended on him and I was able to talk about my morning with my friends. This was without a doubt the most emotional day I had experienced for some time, which was saying something.

#MikeyMonday
Me: How was school?
Mikey: It was really bad.
Me: Oh. Why?
Mikey: Well I kept on laughing and that made me cough.
Me: That's no-good mate.
Mikey: Yeah no more laughing for me at school, I just won't go there.

At age six, when he began school, Mikey had very limited functional language. He would push other children if they got too close at the wrong time. He was not fully toilet trained and was prone to escape at every opportunity. Unlike most schools though, writing this on the enrolment form and discussing this with staff didn't cause any sense of panic or even unease. I was met with care and understanding. Together we developed a realistic and achievable action plan for Mikey's time at school.

Mikey was initially put in a class with other non-verbal kids. I remember being flabbergasted when his teacher sent a note home with his first 'reader' to practice at home. I couldn't believe they were attempting to teach a child who didn't talk, to read. To my absolute astonishment when I sat down with Mikey that night, he was able to read most of the words in the book. Now he had probably memorised some of the words due to repetition, and he definitely couldn't then use them in a sentence, but the point is they didn't let a little thing like 'speaking' get in the way of his learning.

They looked at my child and saw the possibilities rather than the limitations. They saw what could be improved on and not all the problem behaviours the rest of society saw. They created a predictable, consistent, creative learning environment that enabled my son to grow and develop at his pace.

I honestly believe that it was this safe space where Mikey spent his days that enabled him to blossom into the young man that he is today. Mikey enjoys friendships with kids his own age. Mikey has learnt mathematics, language skills, life skills, sports and the list goes on. He has been given so many opportunities and has been able to try new things.

#MikeyMonday
Mikey: I'm never getting married
Me: Why not mate?
Mikey: Cause married people have sex.
Me: What's sex?
Mikey: You know that song 'sexy and you know it'?
Me: Yes
Mikey: Well that's what sex is and that's yuk
Me: ....

I had countless speech therapy sessions for many years with my boys. My awesome Speech Therapist Kerry and I often talked about what the kids were doing, and what we could teach them next. She made a point of always reminding me that we can only deal with the now. I would say things like, "Do you ever think Mikey will be able to drive a car?" She would always patiently listen, then gently remind me that no-one knows what's in store for anyone's future and worrying about it now will achieve nothing.

When Ben was about four, we were waiting for our therapy appointment. He lay down on the floor, feeling tired and overwhelmed, said he couldn't do it today. Kerry walked out and saw Ben. She immediately and wordlessly got down on the floor next to him and copied his posture. Ben looked at her confused then looked away. He lay for another thirty seconds and looked back again. He seemed baffled by this unexpected turn of events. He thought about it for a few seconds, got up and walked into the therapy room and said "Well we start now?" It was a brilliant way of motivating Ben.

Kerry literally got down to his level and let him take the lead. Ben had the best session, as it was about the now. It didn't matter how long Ben lay there, he needed to feel calm and in control. Kerry wasn't thinking about what she needed to get done that day with him, just that he wasn't ready yet.

Kerry came to visit my home when Mikey was two years old. Mikey had a big obsession with Ice Age at the time and he watched it constantly. Often rewinding the same scene or special feature over and over again. Kerry attempted to engage Mikey several times, to no avail. Ice Age was just too exciting. She watched him flap and dance around with joy watching all the characters. I became very stressed about the situation and wasn't sure what to do. I reluctantly suggested turning it off so he could attend to the session. Kerry asked me what would happen if I turned it off. I explained that a huge meltdown would occur and Mikey would be inconsolable for hours.

Kerry asked me if he needed to hear it or just see it? I had never given that any thought. I turned the volume down and Mikey was unaffected. Kerry calmly said, "Well at least now that's less offensive for you". She saw Mikey's pure joy at watching this show and my extreme frustration at having to hear it repeatedly. Instead of insisting he engage with her, which would not have happened in this environment, she helped both of us learn to cope with our day. Mikey remained in his happy state and I was relieved the noise level dropped. I felt a certain weight had been lifted from my shoulders.

Kerry gave me permission to accept Mikey's special interest rather than try to distract him from it. She allowed Mikey and I to enjoy the session, without feeling like we should be teaching him something else. In time, Mikey was able to interact and learn in his speech therapy sessions. He was never pushed too hard and it was always at his pace. If I didn't have this valuable input, I would have continued to judge myself every time the TV was on 'too long'. I would have seen it as a 'cop out' rather than a great thing to do.

Many parents of kids with special needs have been told what their children will be able to do when they are older. I'm glad I was never told 'no, he won't do this'. The fact that I was taught to take each day as it comes filled me with the hope I needed to make it through the tough times. My kids have amazed me in so many ways. I still don't know if Mikey will be able to drive a car, but I know worrying about it now will achieve nothing.

#MikeyMonday
Mikey bursts into my bedroom at night in a big rush.
Mikey: Excuse me mum. Just got to go to the toilet
cause you know, I've got a situation here.
Me: No worries Mikey.

I went to a friend's house one day to celebrate her forty-something birthday. As we clinked glasses, the conversation quickly turned to the old days and what life was like in our thirties. The general consensus was a reversal of the clock was preferred in the group. It took me two seconds of thinking about life in my thirties, to share that I would not turn the clock back under any circumstances. I was so vehement with my opinion. There was a hush in the room I hadn't intended. The answer was simple. I spent the entirety of my thirties toilet training.

Most parents will agree toilet training is not the best part of parenting. With all the washing, wet floors and smelly shopping trips, it's not hard to see why. For me, toilet training went something like this. Jarod learnt to pee on the lemon tree at two and a half and found the toilet on his own after that. At almost three, Ben did his first wee on the toilet, whilst visiting me in hospital after I'd just had Mikey. They both just naturally night trained and the whole experience was quite uneventful.

When Mikey was five and David was three a friend sat me down and told me I needed to train David. I struggled with this initially because I hadn't yet trained Mikey. I didn't want to deal with the heartache of training a child younger than Mikey, thus highlighting just how disabled he was. She was right though. David was trained within a relatively short period of time.

Then came Mikey....

As Mikey was non-verbal, he expressed himself mainly by dragging me by the hand to the item he wanted help with. Mikey was extremely active and enjoyed the muscle tone of an elite athlete. He loved to take all his clothes off anywhere he felt the urge, in any environment and any weather.

I think it was about a two-year period where I dressed Mikey in an all in one bathing suit, which zipped at the back and/or a pair of overalls. When combined, this outfit was hard to remove and as such it was easier to catch him mid undressing. This wasn't as important at home, unless he'd done good old number two's.

My parents were babysitting and had put Mikey down for his nap without the suggested clothing on. They later entered his room to not only find he hadn't slept at all, but he had in fact done number two's. He had rubbed it over every surface in the room. It was in the carpet, all over his bed, on the walls, clothes and all over him. He was loving the sensory experience it offered. To this day, I am so glad, I didn't get home until after they had cleaned it all up!

As he got a bit older the short-sleeved suits were not enough and I had some made for him that were full body length. Try as he might, he could never get these suits off and wore these mainly at night. I could be sure his room would never again be painted with the brown smelly stuff.

Toilet training was a huge process. It involved planning meetings with all the professionals' involved, visual images throughout the house, a personalised book, a video and a list of pictures in order of what was required of him when he went to the toilet. We even had real pictures of his brother (no face) urinating so he could see exactly what he was to do there. I then had a calendar on the kitchen wall counting down how many days he had left in nappies. I counted down a full month before I even started to train him. I walked around the house saying "wees and poos in the toilet" at various times throughout the day. It was a massive enterprise for our busy family.

The first day of training I showed Mikey that the calendar had hit the right day and took his nappy off. Unfortunately, all the pre-planning didn't seem to have made an impact on Mikey. He continued to wet his pants at regular intervals. I enlisted the help from our local Autism travelling teacher service. The teacher spent one week with us with the sole goal of toilet training, or even toilet timing him, meaning going at the times he was taken rather than when he had an urge to do so. She would give Mikey water to drink and took him to the toilet every half an hour. Mikey flat out refused to urinate on the toilet. We realised quickly that he knew what was expected of him, but just didn't want to conform. For days the worker literally followed Mikey around the house. As soon as her back was turned, he would wet his pants. He knew that if she caught him. He would need to be in the toilet, so he 'snuck' his wees.

One day the teacher, being the awesome professional she was, made sure to never take her eyes off Mikey. He didn't wee from eight am to six pm, even though he'd had over three litres of water throughout the day. His amazing ability to find loopholes wasn't lost on all of us. We were in awe of his determination and focus. He knew he wouldn't be doing anything wrong as long as he wasn't wetting his pants, so he just didn't do it at all.

I can't remember how long it was before Mikey made the decision to wee on the toilet. I know he tried for a very long time to avoid it. He would find his night nappies and follow me around the house shoving them at me to try to get me to put them on. I felt like "wees in the toilet", was sort of a mantra I said a gazillion times a day, in the hopes that one day it would click.

Unfortunately for toilet training to occur, Mikey needed to be in clothing that he could easily pull down for the toilet. This also meant when he did poo, he had access to the amazing Play Dough like substance that he had made himself. I don't think there is a surface in my home I haven't cleaned poo off and I even went to a school sports once with poo smeared on my top! One-time Mikey had pooed his pants and put the whole lot in the washing machine. I hadn't noticed it in there and did a whole wash and dry with the poo log.

Mikey eventually urinated in the toilet. I jumped and screamed like I had won the lottery. Never having won tattslotto, I can't be certain it's the same feeling exactly, but I reckon it's got to be pretty close. It was the most amazing feeling of relief. The light at the end of the toilet tunnel got brighter and I had something to build on.

Mikey was eight years old when he pooed in the toilet. I had actually given up trying to get him to do it. I was just throwing out his jocks every time he pooed. I had resigned myself to the fact that he may just never do it. One day Mikey came home from school, went to the toilet and did a poo. I hadn't mentioned anything about it in months, but he knew what to do. He just decided now was the time. I'm sure there was a precursor to the event, but I don't think I'll ever know what it was. From then on, he pretty much always pooed in the toilet. It was only occasionally I would get a smelly surprise in his pants. He wasn't so good at wiping for a long time. But I wasn't complaining.

Mikey became relatively self-sufficient in going to the toilet. Just as a bit of a refresher, I showed him the toilet video he hadn't seen in years. He watched it intently, turned to me and said "If I fart I need to do poo".

Yep. My forties were looking good.

#MikeyMonday
Mikey shoots me in the neck with his nerf gun
Me: Not the neck please
Mikey: Ok I'll shoot you in the leg
David: Why don't you not shoot her at all?
Mikey: I have to shoot her. It's part of my charm

S upport is a word that is often thrown around Autism circles. Mostly the term is used in a negative fashion, when someone is whining about the lack of its availability. Sometimes it is used when describing services available to assist families, but again this often goes along with talks about long waiting lists and minimal help.

The support in the world of Autism I chose to focus on, comes from my friends. I have found this to be a bit of a tricky subject to discuss. I have often disagreed with others in the Autism community, about how much support one should expect. You see, I'm a big believer in all things being equal and relative to one's own situation.

Ben's fifth birthday party was held at a nearby traffic school. The party had a mix of kids with special needs and regular kids. One of Ben's Autistic friends had a lot of difficulty communicating with other kids. He went up to them, pushed them over and bit them. The mum, a lovely and caring mother, instead of intervening with the child and tagging him, chose to go up to parents after an incident had occurred and explain his Autism. Expecting support in this situation is tricky, and I wonder why it is expected in a situation of violent behaviour.

Mothers tend to instinctively go into protective mode when their children has been injured by another.

We as humans all have access to, and experience the same range of emotions all around the world. We all cry, we all laugh, we all yearn, we all love. It's our personal situation that triggers the intensity and consistency.

For example, you often see pictures of kids walking down dirty streets with big containers of water bottles on their head. They travel miles every day just to get dirty water to sustain their family's lives. If someone like me was placed in a situation whereby, I needed to do this just to get water I would undoubtedly have an extreme emotional response to this task. I cannot fathom what life would really be like to have to maintain this existence every day. Why do I bring this up? Well in many ways, to others, I've carried that water too.

Years ago, I took my boys twice a week to the local Playgroup. It was a fantastic opportunity for me to get to know other parents and carers, as well as for my children to socialise and be with kids their own age. Although on the surface that seemed like a great idea, Mikey didn't really agree. Being non-verbal and three years of age he would scream and try to drag me to the gate to go home. He would continue with this behaviour for the first hour we were there. This was not uncommon for Mikey in new environments. I chose to 'ride it out', because I knew he would eventually calm down and the whole experience would be beneficial for him in the end.

Unfortunately, the other mums didn't necessarily know how to relate to my theory. It was really hard for them. Firstly, the noise level was excruciating. Secondly, when a child screams it is a natural reaction to either scatter or stare. Thirdly, people just simply didn't know what to say to me. I was glad at that time I lived life mainly in 'robot mode', because I'm sure the despair I felt would have brought me to tears on a regular basis otherwise. I pushed back any negative emotions and replaced them with a dogged determination to complete the mission at hand.

I'm sure many people cared for my plight and felt for my situation, but they weren't carrying the water. I understood that. I knew in my heart that if roles were reversed, I would stare too. It would not be from a lack of care but feeling overwhelmed with what to do about it. I actually don't remember a great deal about that time. My robot mode was in full swing. It was a difficult period. A friend reminded me that she first met me in this situation.

I had been at playgroup when Mikey did scream to leave.

When they heard the screaming all the other families went inside and left me to my own devices. This friend approached me and empathised it must be hard to do what I was doing. Apparently, I said something along the lines of, "Well it's harder when everyone runs off and leaves you". She then sat down with me. I now laugh at that situation. What could I have expected from anyone at that point? What else could they have done? This friend just sat next to me and we spoke above the screaming. It was so lovely that someone else could see me and my 'water bottle' and attempt to relate to this reality.

I think a lot of people that have kids with disabilities, become frustrated with people that have 'regular' kids. They believe that they should care more and stop whining about seemingly petty issues.

They also believe their children's loud and destructive behaviour should be accepted by others. I'm not so sure about this. I do know that for many years, though, I would mention my 'four boys with Autism' at opportune times to obtain sympathy from people. I even had a name for it 'the Autism card'. I used 'the card' to get into places ahead of time, to get free things and to get preferential treatment at different events.

I won't say I find it easy to hear other people complaining about their kid only getting a 'B' instead of an 'A' in their reports. But I always try to remind myself that it is all relative. They are experiencing the same emotions I did about IQ tests for Mikey.

In my friendship group I was often quoted as saying, "get a real problem". Especially when I became frustrated with what I consider trivial issues in people's lives. It was a coping mechanism, but my choice of words has been to my disadvantage. Sometimes my friends haven't disclosed to me things that are worrying them, for fear they are not 'important enough' to me in my situation.

To be honest, it's hard for me because it invokes jealousy and frustration on my part. For the most part I am never one to expect more support than anyone else, just because I have kids with disabilities. An unequal friendship can wear very thin and exhaust one party.

Friendships need to be nurtured and be mutually beneficial for them to last. I need that. Friendship. Nurturing. Support. Love. Laughter.

When I find myself rolling my eyes at what I consider to be ridiculous issues, I always try to remind myself that I am in fact not the child carrying the water.

Not only do I have, not only running, clean water, I can make it hot or cold at the touch of a button. Now that's awesome.

#MikeyMonday
Me: Mikey what do you want to do when you grow up?
Mikey: Probably live by myself and try not to get fired.
Me: Where will you work?
Mikey: I have no idea.
Solid plan

It's a question most of us get asked often. What do you do for a living? Years ago, my response was easy. I'm a Social/Welfare Worker. Then came the 'mum years'. I initially worked part-time and raised my children, going back to work after each one. When number four came though, I was thrust into another role, the carer. By that stage I had two out of four children with confirmed diagnoses of Autism Spectrum Disorder.

I had so many appointments for therapy, group sessions and professionals. Working outside of the home, was too hard for me. As the years went on, the others were diagnosed and my life took a new shape - what I affectionately refer to as, 'Autism land'. I spent many years eating, breathing and sleeping all things Autism. That was exhausting. I still found that when I was asked 'What do you do?' I was able to proudly state that I was a mother who cared for her children and all their needs. The question became much harder when all the children went to school.

The first year David was in Prep, I separated from my husband of nineteen years, and spent time adjusting to life as a sole parent. The second and third years, I spent decompressing from all those years of ridiculous scheduling and appointments. The year David was in Grade Four, was by far the hardest time in my life at answering the question, 'What do you do?'

Most people have the time and energy to work jobs outside of the home and raise a family. I often judged myself negatively, because I was unable to do this too. A friend once said to me, 'You don't work. You stress'. This is actually a more real description of my life than I would ever really like to admit. I sometimes said 'I'm a mum. I have four boys. I'm a carer'. But the truth of what I did is incredibly difficult to articulate. This is especially so in a social situation, where one is expected to explain quickly what they do. I have gone to painstaking efforts to work 'behind the scenes' with the boys, so when they go out into the world, they are at their best, highest functioning selves.

What did I do? I cleaned. I cooked. I washed. I found faeces in places no-one should ever have to see it. I talked boys out of trees in the pouring rain late at night. I listened to extensive monologues about facts they knew about their topics of interest.

I tried to decipher, from their limited descriptions of events, where a social situation went wrong at school and why they were ostracised from their social group yet again. I hugged them for hours when all they wanted to do was curl up and die. I listened to their anxieties and struggles. I managed their violent outbursts. There are times when I needed a week at home on my own during the day, to recover from being the sole support during suicide watch.

There have been times when I would go weeks without a break. One child or another had to be at home because they just couldn't make it to school. There are times I was overloaded with appointments for the boys. My head got so full and I felt like it would explode. The tricky part for me is when I'm having one of those times with one or more of my kids, people ask me 'how have you been?'. I have to choose between making a joke alluding to the issues or discussing them.

If I chose to discuss it, I hated the look I got on people's faces, knowing I have made them upset too. If I did discuss it, it brings it all back up for me. I therefore often found myself not wanting to talk about things, so I could forget them for a while. I knew people wanted to help. I have always been so fortunate to have all the help I needed. I have services I worked with, I have a loving family and the best friends anyone could hope for.

#MikeyMonday
Mikey appears from the bedroom wearing one of my bras and my highest heels.
Me: Mikey what are you doing?
Mikey: Sorry mum I'm your daughter now.

The more time went by, the more Autism became one of the joys in my life. You hear it a lot that one's greatest losses can become the making of them. As clichéd as that sounds; that started to become true for me and my life.

Mikey asked me once to come into his bedroom to help him with Lego. I gladly helped him press a piece into place and then another. He looked satisfied that I helped him correctly. He says, 'Ok get out now'. It was such a precious moment I broke into fits of laughter. It is moments like that that made me appreciate his life even more. Mikey had no qualms with honesty, openness, and directness and is clear in his intentions. Qualities that I would proudly love to say I possess in full grandeur.

What's interesting was no one seemed to get offended with Mikey's comments. He carried himself in such a way that people find it not only acceptable, but also endearing to hear him say such things. People admire his honesty and respect it. Of course, there would be many that do so out of pity or patronising of him and others because they are mindful of his condition. I appreciate those who did see genuine admirable qualities in the way he conducted himself and enjoyed his viewpoint on life as I did.

#MikeyMonday
Me: You were smiling so that means you are happy.
Mikey: I was smiling sarcastically.

The boys have all been taught to embrace their gifts and seek the joy in their lives. As a result of this, they have achieved so much individually and as a group. Underlying all of this, the Autism is there and has affected everything we do.

I chose and continue to choose to live a life of gratitude. I looked for the gifts and positives life brings. I know that Autism has brought a tremendous depth to my life, which has enabled me to grow in so many unexpected ways.

The main area of growth for me is my mindset. At the beginning I felt feelings of fear, being overwhelmed, frustration and curiosity.

I could see the meltdowns, experiences and lessons needed to happen, to enable us all to learn and grow from the experience.

Sometimes I stopped what I was doing, got lost in my thought and forgot what I had planned to do next. Sometimes I was so focused on getting things done, I shut out all background noise and put all my attention into what I was doing. Sometimes I had so many things I perceived I needed to do, I became overwhelmed and got nothing done. For my kids though, these things that happened to me 'sometimes' are the usual for them. They are the standard. It makes sense to me, therefore, that the tiniest of details are what can cause catastrophic effects for them. Just one conversation too long, one look too confusing, one unexpected thing occurring, has caused detrimental effects and meltdowns.

Meltdowns and shutdowns were always a common occurrence in our home. Some went for minutes, most went for hours and some went for days. I always did my very best to avoid them. But as life is not entirely predictable, so too are our reactions to it. For years, I found myself learning, mostly by feel, how to react when each of my boys lost their ability to function adequately.

There are slight nuances to the way I approached each boy, but there are also some underlying similarities. The one that is most important is the lack of speech required by me.

It took me years of trial and error, to realise that there is nothing I can say to help them to feel better when they are overloaded. They were completely irrational and extremely negative. A lot of people may think silence is something that is natural and are more than comfortable being with someone in that way. I'm not one of those people.

I had to train myself to be with my kids without verbal communication. It took time and dedication. The only reason I persisted was the obvious positive benefits.

When my kids were overloaded they needed to do a few things. They need to let their brain process what's bothering them over and over again. They need to spend time alone, without external stimuli to allow the brain to start to empty itself of extra information. They need to yell, scream, sometimes hit things, or cry to let it out. Then they need me to be there in silence. I validate them and what they are feeling. I empathise without saying a single word. I find that if I come in after they have had enough alone time and sit in silence, they calm more easily and quickly. It is then we can talk.

This may all sound pretty weird to some, but it was daily life to me. What I rarely stopped to think about was the level of emotional upheaval I'm exposed to and take on board every day. It's become so much a part of my life, it rarely makes me cry. I didn't stop to reflect on my day's weight. I then have the ability to judge myself if I don't get things done around the house. I might deal with a major meltdown, then read a book for two hours instead of getting household chores done. Then, to spiral even further I would call myself lazy and hopeless for doing so.

One weekend I'd had enough of my repetitive negative inner dialogue and I went out and did some work in the garden. I felt great that I had finally achieved something. It cleared my mind and my body felt better for it too. It allowed me the space for some reflection. In that moment, I decided, 'It's Ok'. It's Ok if I don't get everything done. It's Ok if I needed to spend time napping and reading sometimes. I needed that. I dealt with high levels of emotions every day. I was constantly acting to minimise or avoid internal conflicts and severe anxiety in my children. But I wasn't doing the same for me. It's OK.

Many of my family and friends say to me they couldn't do what I have done and maintain their sanity. Others have believed that because I didn't work outside of the home, my life was a series of cuppa's and cooking classes. The truth was somewhere in-between. I maintained my sanity by giving myself the gift of time. Time to process what I needed to and time to recoup for the next incident. During that time there were chats with friends. For that I will always be grateful.

#MikeyMonday

Mikey: Mum can you turn the music down I need to tell you something.

Me: Sure

Mikey: You know the black paint sprayed in the shed, well I did that.

Me: Mate that was over 2 years ago

Mikey: Yeah but you thought it was someone from the outside of our family and it wasn't.

Me: I knew it was you mate.

Mikey: Oh well I just wanted to say I'm sorry.

Me: Thanks mate. That's ok.

Mikey was in his eighth year of school and continued to love it. He had always struggled in his extreme need to keep home and school separate. In the beginning he would not allow me to visit him at school. If I did he hid. Later, I was allowed to visit on scheduled visiting days when other parents were there. I could never ask too many questions about school at home and vice versa. He would become quite agitated when people discussed school and home in the wrong environment.

Communication is often an issue with special needs kids, so school sends home diaries every night. These detail anything from what they learnt that day, to an issue in the playground.

Enjoying others perspectives in Mikey's daily experiences, I had always looked forward to reading the diary. If I needed to add a comment on a particular day, I would do so after the teacher's comments.

One year the school introduced new diaries. The new ones had specific sections for both parents and teachers to comment. Loving the new system, I had made a few comments in the diary that were obviously clearly visible to Mikey.

One day I went through Mikey's bag after school – no diary. I asked him about it and he said he didn't know where it was. I was a bit confused but thought that maybe his teacher hadn't got a chance to write in it that day. A few days passed and still no diary. I wrote a note to Mikey's teacher asking if the diary was at school, as I couldn't find it at home anywhere. That night I asked Mikey if he gave the note to the teacher. He said he hadn't, but that he had talked to his teacher about it and she said to look for it at home. A hard target search followed. Still no diary.

Perplexed and starting to get a little suspicious, I got the note I had initially written and put it in a place in his bag where the teacher would easily see it. Mikey saw it, came to me and asked why I needed the diary. More suspicious now, I explained I needed to be able to communicate with his teacher about school. I asked him again if he knew where the diary was. He began to get upset. He brought out last year's diary, saying he didn't know where this years was. I let it go again.

One morning I was doing some dishes and Mikey appears with the missing diary. I was so excited it was found. Mikey immediately says;

"Phew, I thought you would be mad with me."

I immediately responded "Why would I be mad mate?"

"Because I hid it in my locker tub and I didn't want you to find it."

Of course, I went through the "How did that make you feel in your tummy?" thing I always do, when faced with this type of situation. He replies, "Not good". I told him to remember that the next time he goes to tell a lie.

Inside though I was jumping for joy that: 1. Mikey had developed the intellectual capacity to lie; 2. Mikey felt strongly enough about something happening in his life, that he considered deception an option; 3. That he was largely capable of pulling it off; and 4. That he chose not to in the end. It was a huge leap forward for him in his development. For that I was immensely proud.

#MikeyMonday
Me: Mikey, I don't have anything to say for Mikey
Monday this week, what do you want to say?
Mikey: I don't know. Your Mumma is tiny instead of fat?!

I remember the first time I used my first iPad. It was colourful, easy, portable and a lot of fun. I spent hour's researching and downloading apps, books, Internet searches etc. That was just me. The kids of course loved it too. They had educational apps, but they also enjoyed the games too.

It quickly became a wanted commodity in our home and timing the kid's usage was very tricky. But for all the issues, it also saved me countless times. When I first got it, I would take it along to appointments, give it to Mikey who would promptly go under a table and play it.

After spending years with meltdowns over going to new places, all of a sudden, I could go anywhere. This device could do what I hadn't been able to previously. It helped Mikey to shut out the world, while providing the consistency and predictability he needed to change his environments. It was in many ways a lifesaver for me. What wasn't any fun at all was making and overseeing the timetable of use amongst the boys. They all wanted their 'turn' and they all wanted it for much longer than their allocated time. Many meltdowns occurred because of that iPad.

Over the years I attended many conferences intending to learn more about how I could help and relate to the way the boy's brains operated. The conferences of the past were full of professionals working with the kids both on the stage and in the audience. Parents were in the minority and people with Autism even rarer.

I was lucky enough one day to attend an Autism conference where an adult with Autism was speaking. She was brilliant. I felt like I had a bird's eye view into this amazing way of thinking and I was mesmerised. One particular quote she made struck me deeply. I have thought about it on and off ever since. She said "You wouldn't tell a child in a wheelchair they can sit in the chair if they are good, so why would you tell a child with Autism they can have the iPad if they are good?".

That one sentence resonated with me. I decided at that moment I was going to change my philosophy about the purpose and use of the iPad. I told the professionals who had attended the conference with me and all of them immediately raised concerns with the issue. They talked about how a child could get lost in the electronics and not participate in the world. They talked about how some parents might use the device as a babysitter. I listened to their fear politely. In my gut I knew they meant well, but they didn't have Autism and as such were not authorities on the topic.

I knew her message was right for me. I was going to test her theory out.

So, I went home and I saved and saved. In time I had bought an iPad for each of the boys. Now that there was one each, I was no longer forced to be in the position of scheduling time on the device, so I made them unlimited.

Of course, my kids were required to go to school. Jarod and Ben went to work. Some went to sports. They all had chores they needed to do for pocket money. Other than that, I didn't mind how long they spent on their devices.

My kids needed to learn to share. But that is something they struggle with all day at school. When they got home, I tried to minimise the need to 'share' in preference of better functioning kids.

Long ago I learnt the theory that the Autistic mind is like a balloon that slowly gets filled during the day at school. So many things to do, learn, remember, people to work out and interact with. At home I was taught I need to help to deflate the balloon to avoid the point of popping.

This was done in my house largely by electronics. There is something incredibly soothing about a game or video that is repeated over and over again. It also helps when they are able to release any emotion they have been carrying through repetition and predictable scenarios.

I copped a lot of flack for this. Countless people often told me that they believe too many 'screens' in kids' lives are not helping their social skills. It required a lot of strength and determination on my part to give it a go and I had many people on the sidelines waiting to tell me they had been right.

Initially I didn't really notice a change in the boy's attitudes or behaviour. As time went on, however, I could tell they began to relax. At home they were allowed to be themselves. They were allowed to do whatever they wanted. In order to release the built-up anxiety from being out in the world.

My kids behaved better socially if they were allowed their decompression time. A few hours on the computer researching their special interest served to invigorate them and make them want to contribute more to the social side of things. And this was just after three weeks.

I won't tell you it was an easy thing. It was not without some 'worry' on my behalf. When Jarod was going through a particularly hard time at school, he came home and spent many hours in his room with his XBox. I rode the wave though and after the phase was over, he reappeared more social than ever.

All of my kids needed to spend time alone. Having devices was often a way to achieve this. Whack on some headphones and the rest of the world disappears. All of the sensory overload drifts away and there is the solitude they desperately need. It also helps to shut out a house full of loud brothers!

The year Jarod got his learners permit, I spent a nail-biting year at the wheel with him. Then, before Jarod had even finished, Ben got his learners permit. Two boys constantly asking to drive everywhere sent me batty.

I'm not sure how neurotypicals learn to drive but get one of my Aspie (an affectionate term for Autism/Asperger's syndrome) people behind the wheel of a car and their egocentricity could easily be mistaken for extreme arrogance. They thought that because they had read a book, they knew how to drive. My kids are all visual learners, so they do learn from seeing and picturing things. This works really well with book learning, computers and video games. Not so much with things that can lead to our ultimate demise.

I got in the car and for them, it's all about 'signs' and 'limits'. Not the feel of the road and the car right in front of you that just slowed down!! If we could do one hundred kms per hour because that's the limit, why were we doing forty? Well because of the really curvy, wet, traffic filled road son.

It doesn't help either that I was obsessed with getting everywhere 'on time'. I kept forgetting that I needed to leave early if I'm not going to be the one driving. The whole way was spent telling them to slow down, whilst thinking we needed to speed up to get there.

I had an inkling that I wasn't up to the task of instructing, so I sent them both off for professional lessons. After two lessons, Ben begged me to take him out for a drive around town. Thirty minutes later, I was able to breathe again after he went through several give way signs, swerved to avoid nothing and then proceeded to crash right into my carport. I asked why didn't he listen when I yelled "Stop" twice before he hit the post? He calmly answered, "I was easing on the brake like the instructor taught me."

I had thought I was keeping my cool in a lesson after I repeated instructions several times to no avail. Mikey pipes up in the back seat, "Well, it looks like mum is mad with Ben again." I guess I wasn't doing such a good job.

I could handle it when the kids are teaching themselves new things so they take apart something and try to put it back together. When it doesn't go back together, I take a deep breath and move on. It's a whole different ball game when my life is on the line with the new skill being learnt.

Being able to focus well only on one thing at a time is not necessarily a positive trait when learning to drive. Too many distractions and things to remember help to confuse and distract them from their task. So, what do my kids do when they feel this? They sing! Yes! All of a sudden the 80's classics that have filled my kids ears for years in the car, are awesome tunes to belt out. And yes, you got it - They have no singing voice. Any of them.

#MikeyMonday
Me: Mikey, why did you ruin your mask?
Mikey: I did it for the best. I did it for the good.
Me: Hmmmm
Mikey: What if someone put it on and pointed
a gun at ya? That would be scary.

I had a wonderful conversation with a family member at a party one day. We chatted, sipping on our drinks and my eyes were opened yet again. She told me she had read a recent newspaper article I had written, and that some of the information in it was news to her. I explained to her when I have shared, I often feel I have 'depressed' people and I brought the conversational mood lower.

We talked at length about how my family and friends probably want to know more about the things that make up my daily life. My reluctance to share was only evident in my writing. If I didn't write about it, they may not hear about it at all. I guess in many ways, it was easier to write about my life than talk about it.

The conversation did get me thinking though. *How do I learn to share without causing dismay to others? When I don't share, am I only showing one small part of me to others?*

The difficulty I have always had with this, is my extreme wish to live life in the positive. I am constantly focusing on the good, fun, optimistic angle of things. So how do I answer the questions: "How has your week been?" Do I mention the meltdowns? The social issues?

The tears? Or do I talk about the achievements? The mathematical brilliance? The help I get with technological issues? The love? I have always chosen the latter. The conversation enlightened me to the fact that I have had a whole other life I kept from people. I did so with good intentions, but it has had an effect on my relationships with others.

Some only saw the 'fun' me with a drink in her hand and a joke to be told. The loud crazy person at the party, who just can't find something 'appropriate' to say to save herself. At those times I have 'saved up' all my excess energy and just need to release and let go. I don't want to be pitied, empathised with or avoided. I wanted to have fun and enjoy the night ahead.

As with all people though, I go much deeper than that. My life is so much more intense than the 'fun me' would have you believe.

I am a particularly positive person; however, some others are not so much. When I once talked about the suicidal thoughts all of my children have experienced at various times, that is what they related to Autism. That is nowhere near the full picture. *Do I need to give others the benefit of the doubt and not filter it for them? Are others big and strong enough to hear it all, without the blindfolds I put on them?* These are the questions I guess I never really found a straight answer for.

#MikeyMonday

Mikey and I were enjoying a cuddle when the phone rings.

Me: Hello

Mikey: Mum we were having a moment and you kinda ruined it.

So I mentioned I had a disastrous Mother's Day one year. I ended up in tears. High expectations and no preparation can do that.

The next year, needless to say I was determined to enjoy the day. I knew the younger two boys had Mother's Day stalls at school and I would contribute money to cover their gifts. It was the bigger two I needed to work on. With my Autism 'cap' on I realised hints were useless, so weeks before the day I said, "Mother's Day is coming up. I would prefer not to have a repeat of last year." I then went on to say that as they are both working outside of the home, they could afford to plan and get me a small gift. Yes, I did do and say that! I hadn't done that last year and was disappointed.

'Hint' received, I relaxed for a bit. The night before I laid out wrapping paper, scissors and sticky tape on the bench and indicated they were there if anyone should need them. They agreed that they did and proceeded to make a ruckus in the kitchen, while I was ordered to stay in the lounge room so I wouldn't see anything.

The day arrived and I'm awoken with breakfast in bed. Winning! The gifts were a plenty and the handmade items were really special. Of course, I was holding my breath to see what the older two came up with.

Unwrapped, a voucher is placed on my lap – what is it I wonder? Upon closer inspection I have been granted a $50 Netflix voucher. "Wow," I thought. Not only did they spend a reasonable amount each, I might actually like this gift. A part of me couldn't help but be questioning at the same time. Why this gift? Why would they want me to have it?

New to Netflix I asked the boys to set it up for me. Of course, they were glad to do it. My suspicions increased. This was not normal behaviour. Once it was all set up and I was watching my first movie, the catch was revealed. They were able to use this gift too! In fact, I get less free time on Netflix so they can use it. The boys chose the 'premium' option so that movies can be streamed on four devices at once in our home.

When I realised this, I laughed to myself. They did spend their own money. I did get a reasonable gift. They set it all up 'for me'. It really was a bonus, as we all spent the day streaming movies. I was able to leisurely crochet in front of the fire doing it. There was only the one time that all four boys were streaming something different and I was kicked off being the fifth person. Just a smidgen of arguments followed that given it was my gift, I should be one of the four that got to watch it.

#MikeyMonday
Me: Mikey why do you want to have your own room?
I thought you liked sharing with David.
Mikey: I wanna move away from smart boys.
Smart boys are the enemy of funniness!

S tress. It's a word bandied about by people, often referring to things that happen in their daily lives. But what is it really? For me, I found that I could describe myself as stressed when I could no longer function. When there are so many things swirling around in my head, I couldn't possibly fit another thing in. Others might say I operated daily on a level of high stress that I considered 'normal'.

In times of considerable stress, I needed to sleep in order to recharge and revamp my body to work again. This skill/coping mechanism had served me well over the years. By closing down, I had the energy to get back up again to deal with the situation at hand. Otherwise I'd create a further situation to deal with by my behaviour, thus making it more difficult and somewhat circular.

I was actually travelling along well one time, enjoying the glory of a meltdown free week. Then something happened and I wanted to cry instantly. It got me thinking. I might be a little like a loaded gun. Walking around ready to fire at any moment. My 'normal' is elevated.

I got some news on the medical front, that was not really drastic and not life threatening, but still threw me for a loop. I think it was a bit of a 'straw that broke the camel's back' situation. It was the last in a long line of 'issues' I've been carrying around.

I spent two days in my own little bubble. I sat in my lounge room watching TV and staring blankly. I cried or I expressed exasperation that anyone could ask anything of me. I was unable to interact with the world. I was essentially unable to function on more than a base survival level. As luck would have it my kids went to their fathers for the weekend so I had the luxury of allowing myself this space and time.

On day three I was somewhat able to think. It occurred to me that I had, what I would term in my kids, to be a meltdown. Followed quickly by a shutdown. Now I'm sure there are different terms for what I experienced. You could maybe even call it a bout of depression. But essentially, I was unable to function normally. I shut the world out and recharged.

One of the things the boys talk about from time to time, and have happy memories of, is the only time I ever hit Jarod.

Jarod was having a hard time at the beginning of high school and often came home overwhelmed, anxious, stressed and angry. At the time he felt the best way to release this stress would be to take it out on his brother. Sometimes Ben would do something to trigger Jarod but often times Jarod would invent something so he could have a focus for his anger. Even though Ben had a black belt in Taekwondo, he would never retaliate.

One day Jarod started choking Ben and repeated requests from me turned to demands, which then quickly proceeded to screams at Jarod to stop this behaviour. Normally at this point I would jump on Jarod's back and tackle him to the ground, giving Ben time to get away. That day I was nursing a broken rib from a dancing incident the week earlier. I was unable to physically intervene. Instinct took over, and with my good side, I got my arm into a karate chop motion and just whacked Jarod on the shoulder.

The disbelief in all of us was apparent and the shock kicked in immediately for us all. Jarod, Ben and I all immediately sat down in the loungeroom and were silent for over forty-five minutes. I don't think any of us could believe what had happened.

The only other time I remember hitting one of the kids was one day when Mikey was in playgroup he kept squeezing and wrecking all the new textas that had just been purchased at a great cost to the playgroup. I tapped Mikey on the shoulder in frustration. Mikey didn't even notice I'd done it and kept colouring.

Although I had no interest in repeating the experience, it really helped me to understand and empathise what my kids go went through when they became overloaded and just want to lash out. It is something that is out of one's control. It was a timely reminder for me not to push my boys to do chores, homework and participate in social situations, when they feel this way. It was too hard and can lead to a longer time of limited function. Another gift to bring me closer to my boys.

Mikey: Mum try and keep your language in your stomach today.
Laughter ensues.
Mikey: What? I just don't want her to swear in front of all her friends today.

As was common in my household, we experienced a myriad of emotions on one day. Ben was on cloud nine after a very successful teens camp for those on the Spectrum. Then Ben came crashing down. He experienced social exclusion on the bus ride home by some school 'friends', he had seen in the city. It made me wonder why these things seemed to happen to Ben? Why can't he just remain on his camp high for more than an hour afterward?

The thing I found most difficult was he wasn't being bullied or teased. It was simple exclusion. A conversation was being had on the bus that he leaned in to listen to. He was promptly told this was none of his business and summarily dismissed. As a parent I have no power to go to his school and 'deal with the issue', as nothing happened that would allow for this. In the same breath I know for Ben, everything happened. He felt rejection, humiliation and embarrassment all in one swift blow. He felt it hard because he was coming down off such a high from the weekend. In one small moment, Ben went down.

Now my usual practice when something like this happens is to focus on the positives e.g. the camp. This time though I took a quick trip down memory lane and remembered in too much detail what it felt like to be excluded in high school. I just couldn't do it. Instead my somewhat inappropriate response was, "That fucking sucks!" Ben agreed and I let it go to discuss other things.

Two hours later, he came out to say goodnight and he gave me a big hug with it. He thanked me for all that I do for him and for understanding. I told him I'm happy to help anytime and reaffirmed that he is worth it and he is an awesome individual. He heard me talk like this often and I'm sure appreciated it on some level. What he didn't hear very often is the vehement agreement with which I shared his social pain and that's what I reckon I got the hug for. No regrets there on that front.

#MikeyMonday
Mikey: Well there is something in my head I shouldn't say
Me: Why mate?
Mikey: Well... Nah never mind
Me: Is it swearing?
Mikey: Sighs Yes
insert sad face and a long pause
Me: Tell me what's on your mind mate
Mikey: Well, why is fruit healthy, it's a piece of shit?
Yeah, I had nothing for that one. I did ask him to tell me so ....

A great friend and mentor asked me once how my writing was going. I told her I'd been having some struggles of late as I had been feeling low and I didn't want to write anything that wasn't uplifting or positive. She offered me some great advice. She reminded me that things that truly feel wonderful oftentimes come from a place of deep learning, adversity, pain or loss. She said if I didn't write about the pain, I'm only telling half the story. She described the situation as that of a snake shedding its skin. I have built up a thick skin and it was time for some of it to come off.

I needed to go to the doctor. Again.

I looked down at my fidgeting hands and found myself unable to look into my doctor's eyes. I had to get out what I needed to say but I just couldn't watch her reaction while doing it. I guess I had a fear of judgment from her. Even though I know depression is something she would see almost daily, for me it was overwhelming and I was embarrassed to admit that. Even after all those years and going through the ups and downs many times, I still felt a sense of discomfort admitting it. But admit it I did and that's when it hit me, I was grieving. Again.

You might be surprised to hear the grief, years later, was largely related to the kid's diagnoses. When Ben was diagnosed, I had a four-year-old and a six-week-old baby to care for as well. I saw it, but I had no time for feelings. I built up a wall around myself and trudged out into the Autism wilderness. My world was their world. It was full of appointments, therapy and sleepless nights. I can't remember complaining too much about anything except the sleep. I hated losing that. I can remember telling people I feel like I'm a robot. I was able to function relatively emotionlessly for many years.

Now that I had the time to feel, I was slowly but surely letting it all pour out. Sometimes it came in dribs and drabs. Other times I became so overwhelmed with emotion the tears flowed freely. To be honest, although it's gut wrenchingly difficult, I did prefer being able to feel. I felt more human, more healthy and true to myself. What I found hard to admit was that I had to grieve at all.

I was truly blessed to have such wonderful children in my life. Without their special needs, I wouldn't be the person I am today.

So why did I need to grieve at all? Maybe it was the Autistic part of me that needed to grieve? The part that thought life would go one way, but did a complete about face and went another? Maybe I was grieving an 'easier life' that I have perceived others to be leading? What's interesting was that on an intellectual level, and an emotional one to some extent, I knew that everyone has their own battles and issues. 'It's all relative' and I believe that to be true. We all experience a myriad of emotions in our lifetime, it's just different things that precipitate them.

So why did I grieve at all then?

I grieved the need to constantly be going with my own flow, which was often against the flow of society. To enjoy my kids quirks and interests, I needed to set aside societies expectations of propriety, what's acceptable and what's 'cool'. I often came across people who say 'Isn't it good your kids won't go out to parties and get drunk?'. Although I agreed with them, it's harder to admit that I also yearned for them to have those experiences.

Why on earth would I want that I asked myself?

Because it's familiar. Because it's 'normal'. Because one would feel less different to the rest and more like everyone else.

It's like I was fighting myself in a battle of acceptance. I wanted to disallow myself the grief, because I was angry that I should feel any negativity at all about my life. I know my life has offered me so many gifts, learning opportunities and love. Yet I have a small part of me that wanted it to be different. A part I wish didn't exist. A part I was embarrassed to admit was there. It made me feel like a fraud when I talked about how good my life was. But also, because it hurt and I didn't like to feel pain.

I guess it needed to be there though. My life did turn out drastically different to how I would have expected it. And it wasn't all good. There I've said it. I think I will forever wonder why I find it so hard to admit I have had a grieving process at all. I think that's because it has been such a positive and rewarding experience in the end. I needed to grieve my own limitations and insecurities so I could open myself up to so much more in life.

#MikeyMonday
Me: What do you want to say on Mikey Monday this week?
Mikey: I don't know. Mum is weird! I know, tell them I can wear 4 bras!

In 2015 I celebrated my use of a washing line. Yes, you heard right. Let me explain. Rewind eleven years. I had a small baby, a two-year-old severely Autistic boy, a five and a seven-year-old. Times were tough. I literally had my hands full. Due to Mikey's absconding and violent behaviour's, I lived very much in constant 'surveillance mode'. When he wasn't locked in the house with me, I had eyes on him at all times. Alongside this, I needed to watch Mikey with his brothers, as he had a tendency to bang them on the head a lot. With a defenceless newborn that was tricky. For a long time, I enjoyed doing things like going to the toilet holding a baby (the wiping is not fun let me tell you), showering in one minute and of course I learnt to use the dryer.

At that time, it was just 'too hard' to hang out the washing and watch Mikey and David to make sure they were both safe. So, as you can imagine, the dryer became my best friend. Ninety-seven percent of our clothes were all chucked into the machine together, regardless of colour or texture, and cold washed. I wasn't concerned with stains on our clothes, as I was just happy to wear clothes that weren't covered in poo. Almost everything was thrown into the dryer to dry. It was quick, easy and took away an incredible amount of time and stress from my life.

So as is often the case with me, something that formed out of necessity became a habit. Fast forward to early 2015. I was still using my dryer for eighty percent of my washing. A huge change came about two months later when I decided to purchase a portable clothesline. I was not ready to use the permanent washing line as the idea of running out in the rain and grabbing all the clothes, just wasn't something I was interested in doing just yet.

So, I decided to re-join the thousand-year-old custom of using the sun and wind to dry my clothes. And I loved it. I appreciated the fact that I was at a place in my life where I could hang out washing and that's just wonderful.

Mikey gave me a bracelet he had made at school.
Mikey: I thought the colour was girlish and I
had no one else to give it to but you.
Me: How about there is no one else you would rather give it to?
Mikey: Yeah that too...

"Keep Calm and Love Jarod, Ben, Mikey and David"
Mikey wrote this and stuck it on the wall after the two-day meltdown I suffered. Thankfully me 'losing my shit' was a rare occurrence in this household. But it was enough to prompt Mikey to remind me why I do what I do, why I carry on and how my kids are just uniquely awesome.

Obviously, Mikey got the idea for the sign from all the social media variations. But I think it's interesting that he chose this to say to me that day. Keep Calm. It's what I have often found myself saying to the boys when they are becoming overwhelmed. Breathe and calm down. Stay calm. What is calm anyway? Is it a state of being or is it a mirage we present to the world?

I know for me it is a bit of both. My mother often told me I have the patience of Jobe (who is a biblical character with patient qualities). I often wondered though, what that really meant. My meltdown proved that it's that I had a whole lot just bubbling under the surface, waiting to fly out at a moment's notice.

I guess as is often the case, I see myself differently to the way others do. Maybe I'm seen as patient because I rarely outwardly explode. But maybe what I thought and what people saw, didn't always match up. For example, I have found myself in a situation of a clash of minds many times with all of my children. It involves me asking them to do something and them saying I hadn't asked at all.

Now looking at the situation intellectually with a clear mind, it's probable to assume that the kids didn't hear what I said. At the time though, when I repeatedly repeat instructions, I found that hard to see and I became frustrated.

What particularly 'gets my goat' is that they invariably said, "You didn't say that". This causes the indignant part, instead of the logical part of me, to react and argue profusely that I did in fact say such and such.

It is actually a very interesting phenomenon and probably common in Autism. The kids aren't actually being arrogant when they insist I haven't said something. They just can't perceive a world whereby if they didn't hear something and that maybe it was said anyway.

They lack the theory of the mind skills to 'put themselves in my shoes' and imagine a different circumstance. If they didn't hear something, I mustn't have said it. After all, it feels really horrible to be 'wrong', so it can't possibly be the case. Unfortunately, too often I'm 'under the pump' and instead of understanding this, I also need to feel 'right' and I argue my point. That never ended up well. It just makes all of us feel frustrated and confused. Where is the patience there?

The boys and I were watching Star Wars 3 (Anakin succumbs
to the dark side and becomes Darth Vader)
Mikey: David, two words about Anakin. Anger. Management.

Specificity is the key. I've known that for years. But I kept getting pulled up when I'm not clear on every detail. This was brought home to me in shattering detail after a series of events led to stress levels 'times a thousand' in our house.

T minus five days before the incident. I accidentally put out the recycle bins in the wrong week. They weren't collected so we left them there.

T minus two days till the incident. Ben is asked to do his usual job of emptying both the large kitchen bin and the recycling into the outside bins. Ben comes out and noted 'Jarod', whose job it is to bring in the bins, hadn't brought in the recycling bins. He decides to throw all the recycling all over the ground, where the bin should be, rather than walk the extra fifteen steps to where the bins are because 'that isn't my job'.

Ben calmly gets told that it was me who left the bins out, not Jarod, and that any rubbish will need to be picked up. A meltdown follows where nothing is done at all. The next day again I calmly tell Ben he needs to complete his rubbish job. He picks it up and puts it in the regular bin, filling it up with recycling materials. I do the inward groan and then put it out of my mind.

The next day I'm scheduled for day surgery. I left the boys a list of their usual jobs to do before they go to grandmas for the night so I could recover. Ben's job was to empty the main inside bin and recycling. Jarod's is to do the smaller internal bins and take the outside bins to the street to be collected. I went to the surgery, come out, text the boys and grandma separately that I'm on my way home.

It was then that Ben rang me and informed me he was still at home. Jarod had left him behind.

My gut immediately went into stress mode. I started to feel pain that I wasn't experiencing before. Ben told me that he had taken too much time moving the recycling to the correct bin and when Jarod asked him to do it, he stood there chewing his chewing gum. Ben insists he intended on doing the job and it was in fact Jarod's fault for 'choking' him and driving off on him.

I silently begged the universe for just one day off from the minds of Autism and went home to hide in my bedroom. I was then forced to arrange a lift for Ben to get to Inverloch to grandmas for the night.

From Ben's point of view, he couldn't even think of mum having an operation. He's still indignant that he shouldn't have to take the recycling out to the street as that's 'Jarod's job'.

From Jarod's point of view, Ben had been asked to take out the rubbish to the correct bin. Jarod couldn't do his job until Ben had completed his own. When he asked to do this, he copped 'attitude' from Ben aka meltdown. Jarod, also unable to think of his mother, had a meltdown as he could not control Ben's illogical behaviour. Without any adult supervision to offer alternative strategies, he falls into old childhood patterns of choking Ben.

This behaviour causes both boys to escalate their stress levels. Neither had the coping strategies to calm down and make rational decisions on their own. So, I ended up having to deal with this over the phone after surgery.

They both were able to calm down afterward and apologised to me for their behaviour. I intellectually understood how and why this occurred. It doesn't make it any easier to accept when something so seemingly straightforward and simple, can lead to a series of events that cause so much more stress than is required. It made me wonder if I should have them babysat at all times. These are the same boys that excel in areas of intellectual study. Jarod had been just accepted into University the day before after blitzing his year twelve with very little study.

One of the complexities of Autism is that their brains allow them to excel in complex things, but it is the simple tasks that they find the most difficult to do. Simple things like remembering to eat, to shower, to put the appropriate clothing on, and that their household jobs might need to be slightly different once in a while.

I was glad I'd had a few meltdowns of my own in the not too distant past. (e.g. Mother's Day). This allowed me to relate to the feeling of utter confusion, frustration and irrationality, which helped a great deal in situations like this one.

*I got a tattoo (that my son David had drawn) with all
the boys favourite colours included in it.*
Me: Look at my tattoo Mikey with your favourite colour purple in it.
Mikey: That's not my favourite colour. I just picked a random colour.
It's only permanent right?

I'm not sure if there was an exact time I realised I was very different to other mothers. One time always sticks out in my mind as a sort of a 'light bulb' moment for me.

Mikey was non-verbal in Kindergarten and as such, communicating with him was very tricky, time consuming and frustrating for us all.

Mikey was very unfamiliar and uninterested in societal norms and rules of what was appropriate behaviour. I walked into my kitchen and found each and every surface had been drawn on in permanent marker. Now I had no idea how and where he found the marker. But find it he did. He chose to express himself all over my kitchen.

What surprised me, was my reaction to it. I was proud. Yes, permanent marker is by very definition permanent and thus extremely hard to get off. My kitchen is not a great place for its use, but I honestly didn't think of any of that when I saw the pictures.

I saw Mikey's mind in his pictures. I was able to catch a glimpse of what sorts of things he thought about and his knowledge of the world around him. His drawings were of things I wasn't sure he even knew about, the sun, trees, and people in his life. Best of all for me his drawings reflected a development in his brain that I wasn't sure had occurred and had no other tangible way of measuring. It ignited a hint of belief in me that I wasn't just talking to myself. He was in there somewhere.

I called up the kinder teacher, so excited about what had occurred. She looked at the pictures, looked at me and said "That's permanent marker Kris." I'm like "Yeah I know but look at the detail." She too appreciated the pictures but alerted me to the fact immediately that other mothers may not/could not see the pictures in a positive light. It really had not occurred to me to think any other way. I guess when you are dealing with poo being rubbed into every part of your body and the house, you don't sweat the less smelly things so much.

I did get some heavy-duty chemical remover and removed the drawings eventually. But not before I took photos and the time to appreciate what was before me. A milestone worthy of celebration and joy.

#MikeyMonday
We are pulling into a car park and I needed my
wallet that was in the back of the car.
Me Mikey you might need to take your self belt off to do it
Mikey Oh no that's crazy. But I like crazy so let's do this

For the longest time I didn't have what I see now sometimes as the 'luxury' of a career to distract me from my woes. An 'excuse' to be away from my children, without the guilt a mother carries with her in her purse. I couldn't imagine asking someone else to step in and fill 'my role' as protector and caretaker of my precious souls. As such I cared for them continually. That means when I was away from them it was for 'selfish' reasons in my head.

If I had time away from my kids it was to do things I enjoyed, things I took pleasure in. That's such a gift of course. But it's also a double-edged sword because I also carried the guilt with me. Even if it was just a small amount. In the back of my mind there was always the thought that I should be 'working' like everyone else. I should be contributing to society financially, paying my taxes like a good citizen.

I know that's all in my head. I've never met a person that had called me a bludger to my face for having a government carer payment. In fact, the vast majority of the time, I got the opposite, how do you do it? The truth is some days I didn't know how. I never knew when a meltdown was going to hit me. I never knew what the next phone call or letter will bring or how it will change my family in countless ways.

I never knew when the smallest of decisions myself or other people in my life may make, would cause ripple effects that will torture my children emotionally for months to come.

A great example of this was the grade three swimming sports for Ben. In his school grade three is when you start competing in the 'real' races. At that age anyone who has had regular swimming lessons tends to win the races. Ben, having had weekly lessons from six months of age blitzed all the races in the morning and easily won or came second in all his heats. In the afternoon they had the finals and Ben was scheduled to be in every one of them.

Winning for Ben at that time was everything and he was immensely proud that he had made all the finals. His first race, he hit the starting block, heard the gun and went into a complete meltdown. He was unable to complete the race and was rocking in a foetal position unable to be reached verbally. I took him home feeling the same extreme gut wrenching disappointment he had at what had occurred.

It was the next day when the meltdown had subsided that I was able to get out of him that it was in fact the sound of the gun that had replaced the starting whistle, that had 'set him off.' Before that I was completely unaware of what had occurred for him to have had such a reaction.

The school took the best swimmers to the interschool competition and of course Ben wanted to be one of those swimmers. Sadly, he was not chosen to compete for the school, even though his initial times were better than that of others. He did not win the 'final' race so they chose not to count him in. Ben was absolutely gutted! This decision haunted him every single night for the next six months. He cried himself to sleep most nights reliving the day over and over again.

He was upset with the teachers, upset with the process and most of all upset with himself and his own involuntary reaction to a seemingly simple change. I put on my 'mumma bear suit' and approached the school early on in the piece, as I could foresee he wasn't going to be able to let this go. But unfortunately, my begging didn't work.

To this day I still have to try hard to see it from the teacher's perspective. She would have had no idea the impact this decision was going to have on our lives and for how long. A small part of me still resents the fact that this was one of the struggles kids with Autism shouldn't have to go through. It would have been easy just to whack him in one interschool race and help with his self-esteem a little. But I guess that's what all mothers think. The teachers needed to weigh up the needs of all children involved. My kid's primary school was absolutely brilliant with my boys needs during the years they attended so a miscommunication here and there was just us being human.

Unfortunately for Ben, he needed to learn this lesson twice. He won another swim race three years later, two days after his father and I separated. He was given the winning card, then had it promptly taken from him two minutes later, because his stroke technique wasn't perfect. His class teacher and I were both floored that this had occurred and again we went home in tears. That was a harder one though. I guess the people who made the decision didn't know about the other circumstances.

These, and many other events in my life, have assisted me to continue to see life from a different perspective. Now if someone in the street is rude to me, my immediate reaction is *maybe they are having a bad day*, rather than thinking the worst of them.

#MikeyMonday
Mikey: Mum what are you doing?
Me: Opening your window.
Mikey: Why?
Me: To let in all the nice fresh air on this beautiful day.
Mikey: Oh......well good luck with that.

"I feel the 4th square root of 1500"

Now that's a statement that would not be said in many houses around the globe.

In my house it was meaningful dialogue between a mother and a son, used to describe how he was processing the news of a sudden death of a fellow campmate.

That day, prior to his being informed about the death, Ben had just spent over fifteen minutes starting and not completing any sentences when I asked him how school was going. Eventually he was able to articulate the fact that people tease him jokingly at school and he is hurt by what they say. They assumed, because of his Autism, that he doesn't have any feelings about what they say. So they continue to say things. Ben pretends he finds them funny, when he is in fact hurt. The whole process is exhausting for him. He said, "They think I don't have emotions, like a robot, so it's easier to act like I don't." This has always been a tricky area for me, as I can clearly see both sides of this schoolyard conundrum.

I know the kids Ben hung around with. They were kind hearted, genuine people who wouldn't hurt him intentionally. Ben was a child who took things literally and had many issues with learning how to receive certain statements from people. His understanding behind what they meant was limited, so often he might not even 'get' what they were saying. Other times he got it, but it just wasn't humorous to him. He tried to then give it back to those people. Sometimes he missed the mark and unintentionally hurt them, which of course caused more of the same.

We often heard about the troubles of children with Autism and the relentless bullying. We hear less often about the social nuances that haunt these kids every day in the yard, even when surrounded by positive young people. It was ongoing and exhausting for Ben. So much so, that he had a great deal of trouble talking about it, describing the context and I had to join the dots in every situation.

You can see why it was so much easier to learn mathematics. The square root of sixteen will always be four and there is no other way to take it. No hidden meaning, no extra thoughts or analysis required. It is what it is and it means exactly what it says. Wouldn't the world be so awesome if people were that way too?

So, in case you were wondering, the 4th square root of 1500 is 6.223329 etc. It's an irrational number with no real ending. When Ben was a little boy, I had a feelings thermometer chart that would measure his feelings in terms of a number between one and ten. One was very happy and ten was very angry/complete meltdown. It was very helpful for me to try to avoid meltdowns. He could tell me when he was six or seven and I could initiate pre-determined coping strategies, to actively try to decrease his stress.

Finding out about the death of a child he knew, brought about this familiar technique to describe his emotions. Of course, the added mathematical complexity confused me and I had to ask what the answer was before I 'got it'. That in itself was empowering for Ben as he enjoyed maths. Just the thought of 'an equation to be solved' helped. It was safe, it was comfortable and it was a little distraction in a brand-new situation. Death is something we had thankfully succeeded to avoid in life up until now, so we were breaking new ground with this one. I was sure the 'numbers' would go up and down from there but having them to refer to was a comforting thought for us both.

I was explaining to the boys how I might be a bit short tempered
for a couple of weeks because of the pain of my broken rib.
Jarod: That's understandable. It's stress caused by a biological
factor. An emotion-based coping strategy.
Mikey: Yeah, I'm just gonna steer clear of you mum.

My friends had been telling me for years that they think I am 'diagnosable'. True to Aspie form, initially I thought they were joking. By the time I realised that they actually meant what they were saying, I found myself in unchartered waters. I was a little bit offended.

Now it should go without saying, my friends absolutely meant no offence and loved me inside and out. It's me that had the issue. This was a pill I actually took a long time to swallow. Why? Well I'd been going around for years asking people to accept and love my children for their awesome uniqueness and I wasn't even willing to accept those qualities within myself. *Am I one of those people that can't walk the walk? It's ok for someone else, but not for me. Am I a fake? A phoney??*

Thankfully these thoughts all came to be in quick succession and I was able to 'name and shame' myself, so I could 'get over myself' and see this as the reason. I have such a great bond and understanding with my children. It's why I 'got' their special projects. I had them myself! I also had to learn social skills the longer way and make friendships later in life. And it was a blessing in my life in so many ways. I can say that and genuinely mean it.

However, it was a real lesson for me that there was still a stigma within myself about the topic. My ego didn't like this at all. I had always liked to think of myself as an accepting and loving mother, a bit of an example in the field of how to raise these kids well. So why then did I not want to accept these very behaviours in me? Why did there need to be any shame at all? Is it environmental or an intrinsic genetic need not to be 'malformed'? I'm inclined to think that for me, it was largely environmental influences.

So why was there shame for me? I think it was a complicated answer.

Firstly, I didn't want to actually feel and experience what they did first hand. Seeing it from the outside is traumatising enough. Secondly, if I was caught up in my own issues, I couldn't be there for them. Thirdly, I really didn't want them to suffer the pain I did as a child. I didn't want to remember it. I didn't want to relive it. I didn't want to recall my life as a child at all. It was a lonely, dark place in my mind and I was subconsciously terrified for my children that they would suffer as I did.

So, it was not actually me wanting to be 'normal'. It's more that I know firsthand just how hard it can be to be different. So much so, that I fooled myself about my 'differences' for many years.

The not wanting to be Autistic was more about me not wanting to acknowledge and recognise how hard it was for me growing up. I desperately did not wish that for my children. Intellectually I know it's a different world for them and they had so many more opportunities than I would have had, if I'd been diagnosed. But somewhere deep inside of me, my emotional self wept in fear when one wasn't accepted and loved for who they are.

That wasn't going to be the case with my children.

Here's a little example of why I think this is so. My friends and I were all shopping one day, causally going in and out of shops. I was hurriedly and passionately summoned to a certain shop and told I had to buy 'that mug'. With a furrowed brow I read the contents and immediately knew that was in fact going to be my mug. The mug read

'Fuck did I just say shit'. And even more coincidentally, I had just started drinking hot drinks on a regular basis for the first time in my forty-three years.

'No seriously' was obviously the name of the brand, but even those words rang true for me. I often find myself reminding my children and others around me what I consider to be a joke and what I am 'serious' about. This had come about, because my kids have often been unable to tell when something is a joke.

To address the elephant in the room. Yes, I swear! Yes, clearly, I swear a lot! It only causes me a tiny pinch of pain to admit that I actually said this exact sentence often. At a dinner once, one of my friends' children brought along a swear jar. Needless to say, by the end of the night I had contributed the most money to the jar and the vast majority was from saying the above exact saying.

I of course, purchased the mug and had a little nervous swallow at the idea of bringing it home and my children seeing it. They had heard me swear many times, always in jest and never at them personally. Well not often anyway. Having it written on a mug, I knew instinctively I would be taking it to another level.

Would you believe my kids didn't even bat an eyelid? None of my children even noticed. Why would they? It wasn't to do with them and so it didn't even peak their interest on any level.

Curiosity got the better of me and I tap my twelve-year-old David on the shoulder "What do you think of my new mug?" He nodded up and down and said simply, "Cool". I stared for a bit before I said, "You know that it's got swear words on it?". He took no time at all to inform me "Swear words are just words... it's people that give them bad meaning. Fuck is just another word mum." I was both proud and embarrassed to hear my son swearing so clearly and easily in this context.

I opened my mouth, then shut it, then opened it again. Then I paused. What was I going to say in response to that? As a mother of a child still attending primary school at the time I was fully aware of the inappropriateness of my son using swear words in his everyday language. I knew so many people would judge both my son and myself badly should they hear it.

I'd introduced this language and this mug into my home. The example I was setting was most certainly one of asking him to 'Do not what I do', which made me feel uncomfortable. Secondly, I thought he is right. 'Fuck' is just another word in the English language and we do as a society choose to give it meaning.

In my life many things happen that make me want to say it. It has so many uses, so many connotations and is such a versatile word. It's attractive to me because it serves as a tension release, a soother, an icebreaker, a joke, a way of getting my point across and a way to get others to take me seriously or not. It really is a great word.

So, in the end I just said to David, "I agree mate, but you know most other people don't, so you won't be able to say it until you are older". He just nodded and went back to what he was doing. I was left to shake my head, as I often do at my son's ability to make such a profound statement of learning for me. He simply doesn't have the same 'hang ups' I did as a child.

As most parents with children with special needs might understand, my biggest fear in life was what will happen to my children when I die? I know a lot of people just don't think about it, because it is the scariest thing we will ever do for our children. We are our children's whole world for a lot longer than 'typical' children. Our children take much longer and find it much harder to find their own independent niche in the world. Sadly, some never do. I'm hoping that by saying this out loud more often and writing it down, I can get the courage to face the inevitable planning that is required for my son's futures.

I intended to unlock the potential that is definitely in them and show it to the world. I wanted them to leave the world a better place, because they were in it. They had already done that for this family, their friends and school community, so it's only the wider population we have yet to conquer.

#MikeyMonday
Mikey: I care about fashion I also care about perfection.
Me: What do you mean by perfection?
Mikey: About the people at school and how
fantastic I am when I do my art.
Me: You are perfection Mikey.
Mikey: You know what I mean then.

David came home from school one day and asked, "Mum can we make gingerbread?" For ten full seconds I did the inward cringe and tried to think of a way I could say no without saying, "I can't be bothered".

After that I slapped myself metaphorically and reminded yours truly that these are the exact times I was going to cherish in the future. I wouldn't look back in time and remember the dirty kitchen, I'd remember the smile on my child's face.

So, I said yes. Of course, halfway through the stirring, David's interest is distracted to the television and I'm left to knead the dough whilst eye rolling profusely. After we'd put the dough in the fridge to cool, David reappeared for the 'cool part' where we rolled out and cut the 'men and women'. David loved making the men and women, lining them up and readying them to cook. I flipped again and took my eye rolls back and decided to enjoy the process once more.

The best bit was yet to come though.

I'd taken the three trays full of bikkies out of the oven and within twenty seconds three kids came from different areas of the house. They divvied up the entire batch and started walking away with their goodies.

I looked up from my phone to see Ben and Mikey saying sincere thanks to David with big smiles on their faces. My "oi oi oi" didn't go down as well. I stopped them and asked them what they were doing? I looked at the clock, it was an hour before tea. I couldn't let them eat a heap of gingerbread cookies now, could I? I looked at the three boys and in a split second I decided 'Fuck it' and let them eat them.

It was a wonderful feeling. I went against the unspoken 'good' mothers code of making sure my kids ate a healthy dinner and let them eat homemade bikkies instead. It felt great. For about five minutes, then guilt got the better of me and I shovelled some chicken curry into their faces an hour later as well. No one ever said I was a perfect mother, but I really tried I swear.

Mikey: You know what I did at school that made girls mad at me?
Me: What did you do?
Mikey: I didn't do anything wrong or anything. I just said boys
are awesome. And one of the girls started chasing me cause I'm
so handsome, and good at money, and boys are awesome.

I went to Mikey's school one day for a School Council meeting. I
waited at the front desk for a bit and when no one came, I decided
for the first time in my life to jump the front desk and go into the
meeting room directly. I felt like a 'naughty girl' that just broke the
rules. Which of course I was. What was interesting to me though was,
I wasn't expecting to feel so good about it. I felt great.

So great in fact, I ran into the meeting room and announced to
the group what I had just done. The different reactions where priceless.
But the best reaction of all, was from a school worker who attempted
to scold me for what I'd done and asked me to stop talking about it.
We had a bit of an uneasy dialogue that was masked in humour, before
I ended up letting it go.

The meeting carried on in its usual fashion, but the excited energy
I had arrived with had dissipated. It wasn't until this person left the
meeting briefly that the tension was truly released. It also wasn't until
after she left that another parent admitted she had once done the
same thing and another told me she was surprised at the attitude of

the other woman. As was often the case with me, I was left to defend my actions alone as others don't want get involved.

It was a good lesson for me. I felt what it was like for a child to be scolded every time they put a foot out of line. I even found myself having a child like reaction of defiance that I too easily deferred to in my younger days.

I actually had to say to myself, *let this go Kris, it isn't worth it*. I reminded myself not to take others negativity on board. What would have happened though, if I didn't have those skills and attributes? Would I have taken that one small incident and carried it around with me for the day? It would turn my slight annoyance into frustration, letting it build into something bigger until eventually I lost my shit.

I'm probably sounding a little melodramatic here, but I have seen it happen to others. I have experienced it first hand, the influence one thought, communication, exchange can have on your whole day. If I let the comments in to play havoc with my self-esteem, my ego and my child self, they can spend too much time growing out of proportion and becoming monsters in my head.

So, what did I do instead? I chose to later compliment that woman. I found something she was talking about to praise her for. Why did I do that? To suck up and show regret for my 'bad behaviour'? No, I chose to believe that her comments were coming from a place in her head where she had allowed negative thoughts to fester so much so, that they were overflowing in my direction. I wanted to break that cycle for her and offer her a new line of thinking that would improve both our days.

I couldn't always do that, but when I did, I always felt better. It means I was truly living the authentic life I wanted to. She may have thought I said those things out of remorse for my behaviour and if so, that's ok too, as long and my comments served to uplift her emotions. I can't say for sure because I couldn't go into her head to see, but I think it worked too. People do love to be complimented rather than scolded as a general rule.

#MikeyMonday

David: If you could have any three things in the world, what would they be?

Me: Love, joy and peace.

David: That's exactly what I thought.

Mikey: I would choose rich and famous, very handsome and an awesome dancer.

I was sitting at a pub on a girl's holiday having midday drinks, when I was all of a sudden taken into a trance. The live one-man band started to play the song "Star Man" by David Bowie. Immediately I was transfixed and just like it seems to happen in the movies, the world around me dissipated. It was just me and the song left on the earth.

Luckily my friends just let me go to my 'special place' and carried on talking around me. It was a magical moment. It was so obviously 'a message' for me that I kept thinking about it for weeks afterward.

I purchased the song, printed out the lyrics and played it repeatedly. I couldn't get enough of it. What was 'the message' though? I tried to let it just come to me, but quickly found myself frustrated. It had been such a profound situation and experience, that I wanted the lesson to equal that level of intensity.

Maybe the lesson was when you feel true joy, life can be mesmerising? Maybe it was in the lyrics? Maybe it was a message from David Bowie in his resting place?

I decided I'd go back to the lyrics. The chorus goes...

There's a star man waiting in the sky He's told us not to blow it cause he knows it's all worthwhile.

He told me:

Let the children lose it

Let the children use it

Let all the children boogie

I've always believed that there is a 'star man' waiting for us to take us to the next plane of existence. Whether that be God, Buddha or the Universe to me that's not important. I have and continue to feel connected to mother earth in ways that cannot be adequately explained in any textbook. Things that have happened to me have been nothing short of miraculous. It is my faith in these things that has allowed my soul to soar in the face of adversity.

The star man 'has told us not to blow it, cause it's all worthwhile'. To me a real connection with my emotional wellbeing and the constant struggles that occurred in my head.

It's the next words though that has the most connection for me. "Let the children lose it". When I hear this, I am inclined to bring to mind the many and varied 'meltdowns and shutdowns' my children and I have endured and will continue to endure. I have a somewhat unique perspective on meltdowns. I genuinely believe that they are healthy for us.

Quite literally. I watch my sons get very angry, let it all out and then the anger dissipates and they don't need to carry those emotions with them in life, leaving them to fester and become cancerous in their body.

They can't 'suck it up' or 'chin up' or 'don't' cry', like we are often advised to do. This serves to bury genuine emotions, rather than healthily expressing them and letting them go.

"Let the children use it" to me means let the children 'use' the star man. Call on the higher power inside of yourself and everything around you to build yourself up, reach your goals and fulfil your life purpose. Don't cut the kids off to their own personal connections, which may be different to the way you connect.

I think to me, it also means to learn from the children in this area. Children were born after us and oftentimes we as adults take that to mean the learning goes from adult to child. In things like this, I believe that kids are actually far more 'in tune' to their own inner purpose and souls yearning than adults are.

In fact, the day that I sat down and watched Mikey as he played with a small piece of Blu Tak about the size of a ten-cent piece for two hours, it finally hit me. He is happier than I am. He was experiencing the true joy I had always aspired to have. I was trying to teach him to join me in my less healthy, less happy, more complicated world.

"Let all the children boogie" to me just sums up and completes the prior two lines. Kris, let your children find their niche and dance in it. Encourage the things that they have decided bring them joy and let them run with it. Provide them with the dance floor, which to move about freely, happily and with big smiles on their faces. They will leave the world a better place for them having been in it.

Yep pretty huge for me! Huge moment with huge lessons all wrapped up in an awesome song written many years ago. I so want to be able to 'tune in' like that every day.

#MikeyMonday
Jarod: Say something funny
Mikey: Boobs
Jarod: That's a Mikey Monday for sure
Mikey: No! I didn't say that. I'm not a perv.

"She's not Alien" was the remark from my sister in law when observing a conversation between her three-year-old daughter and me one day. I looked at her confused at first. Then I realised I had been talking in a ridiculously clear halted and simplistic English language. I guess eighteen years of talking to people who don't always understand what you are saying had taken its toll. I saw a small child and assume subconsciously, that they won't be able to understand me without being super clear.

Yeah Kris that's just your kids not 'typical' kids. It reminded me of one time at playgroup when Jarod's only consistent word was 'car'. He said it clearly and he said it often. But that's pretty much all he said for about a three-month period. I had a car crash into the side of my car once. Jarod and Ben were both napping in their child seats in the back at the time. Jarod woke up and pointed at the other car and said 'car'. He was almost two and a half.

We spent at least an hour on the side of the road ringing the insurance company etc. and getting the kids into the taxi to continue our journey. All Jarod said was 'car'. Another girl in our playgroup almost a year earlier would say things like "Ladies and gentlemen, the couch!" Just a smidge of a developmental difference there.

Unfortunately for me, three more kids with delayed speech cemented in my mind little kid = can't talk well so they will all be 'Alien' to me. Even to the point where I would call myself 'mum' or 'Kris'. My kids had trouble with who is 'I' and 'you' as I could be talking about them or me. The third person is the way to be clear on that. And yes, I did say "Kris will send your doll in the mail", in very clear English. Three-year old tend to be very forgiving though. What did strike me though is my complete lack of awareness of this. I told a friend the next day and she said "Yeah I've noticed you do that too". I had absolutely no idea that was what I was doing. I'd become so comfortable with Autism, that it's my normal. I probably do a whole heap of other things I don't even notice. And no, I didn't need to do it for my children anymore either. Just another habit formed in Autism land that had stuck.

#MikeyMonday
David: Mum what bird is that out there
Me: I'm not sure. I think it's an Ibis.
Mikey: I don't care what that is… As long as no one
insults it. They have feelings you know!

I was listening to a podcast with my earphones in when David tapped me on the shoulder and pointed to the lounge room door. I took my ear phones off and ask him "What?" He just continued to point. I said "What" again, before he told me there is a man at the door. It was the wood delivery guy. He was a little grumpy saying he's been knocking on the door for ten minutes and no one answered. Evidently at the other end of the house, the man gained Mikey's attention but all he did was point to the front door and then proceed to ignore the man. Ben in the next room also had his headphones on and didn't hear the man. It was David up the other end of the house that eventually heard the knocking.

I apologised for making him wait and simply said "Yeah Mikey won't talk to strangers". He replied gruffly again that he had experienced that and that it bothered him. He started to explain what Mikey had done and I didn't need to hear it. I've heard that record play many times before. I know what Mikey would have done, he would have pointed to the front door then hidden under his blanket until the man went away.

So, I cut the man off a little bit and said again "Mikey doesn't talk to strangers, it makes him scared. He's Autistic." Well the man went to go on with his gruff explanation of events and paused halfway through when it was clear he has heard me and understood. "Oh, is he?" was all that he could say next.

In order to 'save him' from an awkward conversation I just said again that he doesn't talk to strangers, apologised again and changed the subject. He then went onto say it was probably more like five minutes rather than ten he had been waiting.

That experience was usually one that moved from judgment of my parenting and my son quickly to sympathy. I sub-consciously avoided the sympathy, because I didn't need it and neither did my kids. So instead we moved on. I didn't carry it. I didn't judge the man. He wasn't to know and to him Mikey would have seemed rude and unhelpful. The other two boys and I helped him unload the wood and it wasn't mentioned again.

It got me thinking though, my friends who have kids with disabilities often talk about the judgment they receive from others about their kids and how they act and are treated. I often talked about it as a rare occurrence to me but maybe it wasn't? Maybe things like that are taken as negative by mothers, doing the sometimes seemingly insurmountable task of raising a special needs child. Maybe this one encounter serves to cement their thinking, that the world will never change and accept their child? Maybe they react differently, start to judge themselves and try to train their son to respond to strangers who come to the house in a more socially appropriate way? Maybe this led to a whole lot more stress within the mother and child and snowballs into the next meltdown?

I think I reacted differently because having four children with a tendency to meltdown, I was willing to avoid them at all costs. Sometimes, I guess this could be seen as the 'woosy' way out. Sometimes it was just the smartest choice at the time. Was it really worth making Mikey speak to the man who he sees once a year? Well clearly my answer to that was no, it was not worth it.

Mikey and David are playing with magic sand.
Mikey: I'm going to make my own face and kiss it.
David: You are going to kiss your own face?
Mikey: Yeah, I like my own face. Why wouldn't I kiss it?

I came across a meme one day that advised us all to look 'past the Autism' and 'into the human being' instead. I didn't like it.

I had to think for a bit about why this one quote would affect me, given it was posted in a positive light. I truly believe in acceptance for all on the Spectrum. I realised what my problem was. I don't want to go past the Autism to accept the person. I wanted to accept the person with the Autism.

I think the two are inexplicably linked, Autism and the person. It's when you are looking at the person WITH the Autism that the gifts emerge. The ability to maintain focus on one topic and perfect all knowledge and skills around it. People without Autism simply cannot replicate this. That's Autism and it's awesome.

So, when someone says to me, "So you have four boys with Autism?" with a furrowed brow and a sad face. I reply "Yes I do!" with a happy face and a positive disposition. It's not the easiest life. But in so many ways my life is so much more rewarding than others. Entirely BECAUSE OF the Autism. I didn't need to look past that to enjoy my children. It's because of that, that I could and did, enjoy them.

They were all so talented, honest, reliable and great people to be around. I used to say to others that I didn't choose this life, but I make the best of it. I changed that to saying that my higher self or my soul 'chose wisely'. It was the best thing that ever happened to me. And I meant it. I embrace my kids wholeheartedly with genuine acceptance and appreciation of them as human beings on the Spectrum.

Jarod, after not wanting his peers to know about his Autism initially, eventually grew to love his abilities. When asked if he wanted to disclose his Autism to his University professors as part of his Disability Support plan, he had no trouble disclosing this information. He was told he was allowed to have privacy and that they didn't need to know if he didn't want them to. He didn't hesitate for a second before saying add it in. He was happy for the first sentence to read, 'Jarod has been diagnosed with Autism'. He had no shame attached to his diagnosis, I was so proud of him for that.

Mikey and I went to the hospital for a nasty ear infection this weekend.

Me: You were born in this hospital. Did you know that?

You came out of mummy's tummy in this building.

Mikey: Don't you mean your vagina?

Me: Well.... yes, I do?!"

Mikey: Mum, did you and dad have naked time in May 2001?"

Me: What?

Mikey: Well it takes 9 months to make a baby so I counted
back from when I was born. It was the 21st May 2001.

Me: ....

Six years after the separation between myself and my husband, Mikey talked about it for the first time. I was initially blown away by the question as it had never been raised before. Mikey was mostly non-verbal at the time of the separation. We were driving along in the car and Mikey simply says "Mum why aren't you and dad together anymore?" I answered him in the best way I could, directly and succinctly. I told him sometimes mums and dads fall out of love with each other. He thought about it for a minute then said "O.K.". Not being able to let the moment simply pass by, I asked Mikey what made him think of that today. He said "Just the waiting." He then said something that broke my heart. He said "That's poor mum." I clarified with him what he had said. Indeed, he indicated he was referring to the separation being a 'poor' situation.

I wanted to cry. Why? Because he was right. For any child, their parents separating is a 'poor' situation. It reminded me again that children never stop wishing for their parents to get back together. Six years on and Mikey was able to describe easily and perfectly a situation that is completely out of his control yet affected him so deeply. I internally wept for him and his siblings. The guilt crept in a little.

I then did what I knew was the only thing I could do for him,

I acknowledged that yes it was poor and that sometimes life sucks. I swallowed my own issues and I addressed those of my son. I wanted him to feel heard and acknowledged. Even though I could not 'fix' the problem that I had contributed to causing, I could at least offer him that. I was also able to offer him a clear picture of the future and explain that mum and dad will never be together again. Mikey's answer to this was gold "Is that because dad has re-married?" "Yes". I answered. That was the easiest explanation for him so I went with that. He didn't talk about it anymore.

I had worried that I said the 'wrong thing', not talked about it too much, not talked enough or said something unhelpful. It took a bit to shake it off, but I made myself do it. I knew that if I wrapped myself in guilt, I would be no use to anyone, I couldn't change the past but I could offer the kids a stable, loving and bright future.

As I mentioned earlier, I have had many years and years of hidden turmoil over Mikey's diet. At the age of two Mikey's diet consisted largely of non food items. Mikey's absolute certainty over the foods he chose to eat were based on his own personal set of logic and standards, of which I was rarely privy to. I'd tried many times to predict foods that Mikey may or may not try to eat. I had often been proven wrong as he decided not to have something.

The most difficult has always been vegetables and fruit. As Mikey grew and developed, his foods choices became more and more limited. The only fruit Mikey would eat at home was apples and the only vegetable was a teeny tiny piece of carrot. I tried everything. I tried positive and negative reinforcement. I tried positive and negative punishment. I tried education around the benefits of nutrients. I tried bribery. To cut a long story short, I thought I had tried everything.

So, at fourteen years of age Mikey's food diary would read as follows: Breakfast – one apple puree (full of sugar), morning tea – four shortbread cream biscuits (full of sugar), lunch – up to three large sausage rolls, afternoon tea – more biscuits or a plain bread roll or chips, tea – chicken nuggets and chips. Dessert is more of the same. For years I tried to encourage better eating, while simultaneously giving up. Trying was just so overwhelming and exhausting.

I made the decision that I needed to be a better role model for my children in the area of nutrition. I needed to step up and stop being so half hearted about it all. I needed to focus on me first. A rarity for me.

One of the first things that attracted me to the Herbalife Nutrition program was the formula they use to make their breakfast shakes. It included lots of the vitamins, minerals and nutrients you need for your day. Absorbed at a cellular level in the bloodstream, I thought it would be ideal to have something Mikey could consume that would actually get absorbed by his body. I had to bottle my enthusiasm for the idea that Mikey might, one day, be able to have this and enjoy the benefits.

Why bottle you ask? Well for Autistic kids change can suck. Anything different needs to be slowly introduced and carefully planned, so that it doesn't cause too much anxiety for the person. When my first shipment of products came, Mikey was clearly told they were new foods for me. Not even directed at him in any way shape or form. I then just proceeded to go about my daily life, eating and drinking the products, and occasionally talking about how good I feel. And I felt amazing! Having never experienced dynamic health in my life before I was amazed at the benefits to my mindset and energy.

I knew I would have to simply have the products in the home for a long period of time, before I would even broach the subject with Mikey. I was initially thinking I would wait six months, but I woke up one day after only four months with the urge to 'have a go'. So, I did.

I took a deep breath and pretended to act causal as I said good morning to Mikey. I was scared that if I simply breathed the wrong way he might say no and never try the product at all. Fear almost overtook me, but I gave myself an internal 'you can do it' speech and forged ahead. The conversation went as follows:

Me: "Mikey I'm making some Herbie pancakes this morning for mine and Ben's breakfast, would you like to try one?"

Mikey: "Why would I want one?"

Me: "Because they are delicious, they are really good for you and you wouldn't need to eat your carrot tonight if you did"

Mikey: "Ok can I have maple syrup on top?"

Me: "You sure can"

Mikey ate the whole pancake!!! The universe aligned for me. I finally found something good for Mikey that he would be prepared to eat. And it's so many vitamins and minerals all in one convenient, palatable package.

I then tried to pretend I wasn't hugely excited by the whole encounter and that it was just a day like any other. But to me it wasn't a day like any other. It was a monumental day of hope and promise for the future. I cried and cried throughout the day. Much to Mikey's dislike.

As with all products, individual results vary and on that day all I knew was my son was finally getting nutrition into his body. Little did I know that this would change our family's lives forever. Mikey saying yes to that pancake spurred me to share my story with others and will go on to directly and indirectly impact thousands of lives. Mikey has grown and developed in confidence, strength, is much more assured and calm as a result. The changes in Mikey are documented on my Facebook page called The Gift of Autism and will be the focus of a whole second book!

#MikeyMonday
Mikey: There was a shooting with five people dead
and five injured in the United States
Me: Did you watch behind the news at school today?
Mikey: Yes, I did. It's sad isn't it?
Me: Yes, it is. Do you feel sad about it?
Mikey: No, I had to concentrate and listen instead.

This above conversation is one of the many I have had with Mikey over the years, that I absolutely cherish. It was said as a passing comment so it didn't mean so much to Mikey. He relayed the information as it was for me to receive it. The reasons for this are many.

I am always grateful when I ask the 'right' questions as it gives me better insight into Mikey's mind. If I hadn't have asked how Mikey actually felt, I would not know that he didn't in fact feel the sadness that he attributed to the situation.

Mikey takes information and puts it through a simple processing filter. He decided that he will remember the information, as well as how others feel about it. It doesn't occur to him that others might assume/require him to feel the same way. Also, he doesn't care or notice that he might be judged poorly for doing so. Mikey is unable to process the deeper meaning behind what he had just said. It is magnificent in its simplicity.

He knows it's a sad situation, yet he doesn't feel that sadness. He isn't concerned with the consequences of admitting that to others. Now obviously Mikey's intellectual disability plays a part here, as he didn't necessarily understand the context in which his statement might be perceived. What I love is the natural honesty with which the questions were answered. It makes me wonder how many of us might react the same way but not actually tell anyone they don't feel the 'sadness' themselves either. Or maybe not as deeply as they might portray? It's one of those times that I question why people with an intellectual disability are pitied. We could choose to see their different abilities as a blessing.

Mikey is unable to feel the feelings 'expected' of the situation, as it didn't happen to him. He was given the information in a context of learning. As such he was more concerned with getting the information correct, writing it down and retelling it, rather than relating to the content in terms of his own life. It's not that he doesn't care about the people concerned. It's just that for him he couldn't overwhelm himself with feelings, when he had a task at hand.

I'm glad that Mikey didn't relate to the story. From past experience I know that if he had, he might have lost countless hours of sleep worrying for his own future. Mikey has two ways of processing these tragedies. The first way is by far the easiest for me to deal with as a parent.

I love the fact that he checked with me that, he was correct in saying it was a sad situation. It's like he was confirming he had labelled it correctly. It shows that these things don't come naturally to him and he really is 'guessing' what feelings go with what information.

I love it because I don't need him to know about the tragedy's life has to offer at his stage of development, especially when there is absolutely nothing he can do about them anyway. The only other possible reaction for him is like going from zero to ten. It would be over the top obsession with the topic and letting fear control everything he does. It's how his brain works and I think it's kind of cool.

I wonder how many people when they looked deep inside had a similar reaction to the information? Maybe they felt the sadness when they heard the news. It did serve to change their lives in a profound way or are they just like Mikey and remembered the facts? I admire Mikey's ability to do so unashamedly and that's the biggest difference.

#MikeyMonday
Me snoozing on the couch
Mikey: I kissed you while you were asleep.
Me: Did you? What did I do?
Mikey: I feel the love in you.

I can't remember the exact moment I realised I'd had it all wrong. I needed to learn about happiness from them. I needed to join them in their world so they could teach me. But learn I sure did.

I had spent so much time dragging all my children into my scary, negative world, I didn't appreciate what theirs had to offer us all. The boys had the 'secret'. I started to see my boys in a different light from then on. If they had quirky behaviours or a special interest, instead of using them as currency to get them to have 'desired' behaviours, I took a genuine interest in why they loved them so much. I appreciated them for what they could do, rather than always looking at what made them different.

In short Autism became a gift. My personal philosophy about Autism did a complete flip. I chose to look at it as the best thing that ever happened our family. I was lucky to have had this experience. My whole world changed with this mindset change. The boys could feel that I genuinely accepted them and relaxed in themselves. The boy's self-esteem started to lift, as their talents were being focused on rather than their deficits. We all started to love each other on a healthier level.

This mindset shift meant that meltdowns were just something that happened in between all the goodness. It was no longer the focus of our lives, but rather the background we dealt with and swiftly moved on from when they occurred. I spent a great deal of time watching and learning about how to create my own joy using the boys as teaching tools. They all knew instinctively what made them happy and it wasn't at all what society often teaches us. It came from within not from an external approval from others.

Friendships started to develop and improve, because now that I had a gift I no longer sought pity from those around me. I maintained friendships based on mutual respect and love. I was able to share my kid's passions from a perspective of pride, rather than shame. I was much less concerned with what others thought of it and me. My kids taught me that.

I learnt that as mothers we often say we want our kids to be 'happy and healthy'. We don't usually mean that though. We really want them to be just like all the other kids. In some cases, we want them to be better. We want them to win the running races, have all the friends and be great with their schoolwork. We don't want to say 'my son just loves to flap and jump up and down all day'. When I did start to say that though, I got interesting reactions. Most people outwardly agreed with me, but you could tell they thought I had quietly gone mad. Some saw what I meant but were still quietly glad it wasn't their lives. And a smaller third group actually 'got it'. They became my close friends.

I'll repeat it again. What you focus on in life definitely expands. When you see the good everywhere, the good will be everywhere. There is so much good in Autism. Imagine the freedom the boys must have had when they didn't care what others thought of their behaviours, interests, foods, clothes and facial expressions. Imagine actually only caring about whether you feel happy about something, instead of always worrying about what others might think of you. My boys don't have to imagine that, because they lived it for many years. When I joined them in their 'happyverse' it was a magical place. And what I found was that by joining them in their world, they were then more prepared to join me in mine. That's when the words came and the life-threatening behaviours stopped. We had found our middle ground and thankfully I learned just in time what had been in front of me all along. Pure love.